This book is dedicated to the people of Faith Community Church who demonstrate daily that faith, hope and love are alive and well. Your passionate commitment to God is a living demonstration that no matter what the past may hold, today is a new day and the future is bright.

REGENERATE

TOTAL SPIRITUAL TRANSFORMATION

ACKNOWLEDGMENTS

It is always challenging to take a life-changing experience and turn it into a book. Whatever level of success found here is due to the inspiration, contribution and support of a great team.

First I would like to thank Pastor Dawn Jackson for organizing the structure of the book and authoring the forty-day devotional. This book would not have happened without her.

I am grateful also to the lineup that pushed through all obstacles to turn a manuscript into a publishable book. I am indebted to team leader and superstar Kim Garcia, with key support from Clete Rodriguez, Karina Price, Steve Lopez and Paul Stephens. Thanks too for the assists from Kelly DuPée, Grace Wabuke and Karen Watkins. The Lakers cannot have any of you — you are stuck on team Faith!

Thank you for the office, business and legal support coming from Mel Gaines, Alice Bell-Gaines and Garry Stewart.

Special thanks to Dan Reeve for overseeing the entire project — somebody has a great son! And talking about family, I just know my only daughter Julie Ferrell will give this book the prominence it deserves in the Balanced Living Bookstore.

In this book I have offered a few quotes from friends and members of our church and television family whose ongoing transformations are inspiring thousands. To protect the privacy of the individuals names have sometimes been changed.

Last but not least I want to thank my wife Marguerite who throughout the entire process has inspired, encouraged, edited, corrected and, if I may say so myself, just looked beautiful.

Regenerate has been the most powerful experience in the history of our church — and Faith started back in 1980!

My prayer for you as you seek God and read this book is that you will be changed forever by experiencing Total Spiritual Transformation.

Press on!

Dr. Jim Reeve

REGENERATE

TOTAL SPIRITUAL TRANSFORMATION

DR. JIM REEVE

Published by Jim Reeve Ministries, Inc.
1211 East Badillo Street, West Covina, CA 91790

ISBN 978-0-61560-584-5

CONTENTS

CHAPTER ONE

———————

Dancing Around Goliath

Dancing Around Goliath

Pastor Jim has been talking about "THAT THING" that is hard to let go and get rid of. I am so blessed and happy to say that mine is gone. I'm free from "THAT THING!"
- Christina

It is time to get serious. Business as usual is not going to cut it any longer. It might be we are sick and tired of being sick and tired, or perhaps we simply want something more out of life. Maybe like a cat we feel like we've been cornered. We can't hide. Apathy and indecision no longer suffice. It's either sink or swim, fish or cut bait. Oh sure, we have always planned on doing something different someday, but someday has never come. Until now.

> *Business as usual is not going to cut it.*

David's someday began in the most mundane fashion. Thought to be too young to join the army, he was going about his morning chores when his father Jesse asked him to take lunch to his brothers. No big deal. Not too exciting of a task. Except for the fact that David's brothers, along with the rest of the soldiers of Israel, were preparing to fight the dreaded Philistines. So far, however, things were looking more like a baseball brawl — more shouting than actual fighting taking place. A Philistine warrior named

Goliath was challenging Israel to send their best man to a mano-a-mano duel to the death — winner take all.

No one in all of Israel was willing to face the Philistine warrior. No one dared answer the challenge. Why? Goliath was huge. He was overwhelming. He was unbeatable. On a daily basis Goliath defied the army of Israel causing both king and soldier alike to quake with fear. For forty days they lived with the enemy's taunts. For forty days the giant intimidated the Israelites. For forty days the people of God refused to face their enemy. For forty days they danced around their Goliath.

What is your Goliath? What is it that stands between you and breakthrough? What are you ignoring? What are you denying? What are you hoping will just go away? What is it that rears its ugly head defying any attempt you make to press into a deeper walk with God and experience the abundant life Jesus Himself has promised you? Are you dancing around your Goliath?

What is it that stands between you and breakthrough?

When David heard the taunts of the giant he sensed his someday had come. Unlike everybody else on every other day, he could no more ignore the challenge before him than he could resign himself to accept the way things were going down. Come hell or high water, David decided to do something. SPOILER ALERT! — a divinely empowered David took Goliath down, rescued God's people from fear and bondage, and was thus thrust into his destiny. When his *someday* arrived, he answered the call. Then, and only then, did everything finally change.

Flash forward 1,000 years from the time of David to the time of Christ. Jesus had called, trained and equipped His disciples to minister in supernatural power. It must have been exciting for them to experience a transformation from simple fishermen and tax collectors into world shakers and history makers. Things seemed to be going great until one day they encountered a demon who refused to come out of a little boy who had been brought to them. This was no giant, but a small child they were dealing with. After all attempts failed, Jesus intervened. With a single command He set the boy free. Perplexed and probably embarrassed by the situation the disciples asked Jesus in private why they were not able to cast out the demon. Jesus responded, "**This kind** can come out by nothing but prayer and fasting" (Mark 9:29, NKJV).

Maybe you can identify with the disciples. You have experienced varying degrees of success in your Christian walk when seemingly out of nowhere something arises that hinders your progress and absolutely refuses to break. Perhaps it's nothing new but a lingering bad habit or a stubborn addiction. Maybe it's a long desired breakthrough in your finances or relationships. Privately you have questioned the Lord as to why you can't break through this situation or circumstance.

You are experiencing a *"this kind"* of problem. What used to work no longer seems to be effective. Coping mechanisms cannot mask the pain of *"this kind."* Pint-sized victories and puny breakthroughs can no longer obscure the taunting giant staring you in the face. *"This kind"* does not respond to business as usual solutions. Like the disciples you do not have the freedom to do and be what you want to do and be. You are in bondage.

But I want to tell you that today is a new day! To quote that sage Yogi Berra, "It ain't over 'til it's over." To echo Mark Twain, the reports of your demise are premature and greatly exaggerated. It's time to tell the enemy, "Don't pop those champagne corks just yet! Don't drop that confetti! It's not over. God has not brought me this far to let me down now."

You are preparing to embark on a journey called **Regenerate**, a forty-day spiritual growth campaign that will bring about *total spiritual transformation*. If today you were to take a picture of yourself spiritually, and then really plug into Regenerate, I promise you will not recognize yourself forty days from now. The before and after snapshots will clearly show dramatic change.

Your *someday* is here. Your time is now. Answer His call. Seize the opportunity. If you will dedicate yourself completely to God for the next forty days, pursuing Him with all your energy, you will experience a very personal extreme makeover. No more dancing around your giants, no more pretending and ignoring, no more wishin' and hopin', but, finally, genuine transformation and victory.

Jonah experienced life-changing transformation after being inescapably confined. He had been sent by the Lord to prophesy to the people of Nineveh. Problem was, Jonah did not particularly like the people of Nineveh — they were the avowed enemies of his own people. If it were up to him, he would just as soon see them go to hell as repent of their sins and be blessed by God. Therefore, rather than obey God and go east to Nineveh he headed west toward Spain. Who wouldn't prefer a vacation at the beach to an extremely dangerous journey in the desert involving a task you hated anyway?

At any rate, along the way he was swallowed up by a great fish. The Bible never says it was a whale, btw (that's *by the way* for all of you non texters). Trying to prove to skeptics that a human can live for three days inside a whale seems like wasted energy to me. It was a special fish created by God to get first Jonah, then the entire city of Nineveh, on the right track. If the Creator had wanted to decorate the inside of the fish with a king-sized bed and flat screen television, no cynic on earth could have stopped Him!

The end result of this fish story is that Jonah found himself in a place of confinement. Even if God had made his accommodations as comfortable as a hotel room, Jonah discovered it was just like Hotel California — he could check out any time he liked, but he could never leave. There was no way he could get out on his own. The removal of options to leave forced Jonah to deal with his Goliath.

Regenerate is your opportunity to face your Goliath. Personal habits,

Regenerate is your opportunity to face your Goliath.

hurts and hang-ups which you may have long ago given up on and reluctantly accepted as unalterable are now back on the table as points of breakthrough. For a mere forty days if you are willing to face your greatest fears and give it a go one more time you will experience total spiritual transformation. Jonah did.

From his place of inescapable confinement Jonah discovered the secret to liberation. After all, it is one thing to have life swallow you up, but to come out alive is a totally different story.   Time spent in confinement had allowed Jonah to concentrate on the truly important issues of his life. From focused time with himself and his Maker came revelation. Watch what sets him free. "Those who cling to worthless idols turn away from God's love for them. But I, with shouts of grateful praise, will sacrifice to you. What I have vowed I will make good. I will say, 'Salvation comes from the LORD.' And the LORD commanded the fish, and it vomited Jonah onto dry land" (Jonah 2:8-10, NIV).

No matter how nauseous I feel, I hate to throw up. I'll do almost anything to avoid it. In this case, however, with the stakes so high, I would not have minded being one of the chunks. When all hope seemed lost, God set Jonah free. Jonah's confession contains a few critical keys that unlocked the door.

First, Jonah had to let go. He could no longer cling to his idol — the fantasy of a carefree Spanish vacation far away from the challenging will of God. He was trying to escape life's responsibilities. He was not so much pursuing his dream as he was trying to check out of his obligations. I can relate. Over the years there have been times the ministry seems so demanding that I have fantasized about leaving the hassle of serving God and retiring to some remote beach locale to spend my remaining days in peace and quiet. Thank God I never actually did that. I now see clearly that sooner or later I would have grown weary and bored from my *free* days. What I thought was a dream would have ended up a nightmare.

What are you running from? What is your idol of choice? What drug helps you to kill the hurt from the past and numb the pain of today? Has it already turned into a nightmare? Sometimes we can even take healthy things and through our obsessions turn them into idols — career, hobbies, and relationships, to name a few. We fantasize that the perfect job, or perfect spouse, or perfect locale will lead to stress-free happiness. Unlike a God-given dream, following a fantasy only results in "forfeiting the grace that could have been mine."

Second, Jonah adopted a grateful heart. There was so much to complain about inside that stinky fish. He could have passed his last few hours consumed by what *would have been, could have been and should have been.* He could have blamed God or others for his predicament. Instead, Jonah wisely decided to embrace the proverbial attitude of gratitude. Before anything changed for the better, he made the choice to rejoice.

> *Embrace the proverbial attitude of gratitude.*

Third, Jonah chose to have a sacrificial spirit. Whether time, talent or treasure, sacrificial giving is beyond even the most liberal of giving. Most of us give what we can afford to give, even when the price is steep. Sacrificial giving is giving that costs us. It matters. It means something. It is not merely a generous tip. Why would someone ever give up something so valuable to them? Because they perceive they are giving it to someone of greater value. David said it like this, "I will not take for the LORD what is yours, or sacrifice a burnt offering that costs me nothing" (1 Chronicles 21:24, NIV).

If you are looking for cheap fixes and easy solutions Regenerate is not for you. But for those willing to sacrificially pay the price for forty days I offer an exciting adventure that will change you forever. Quite frankly, not everyone is ready for "*this kind*" of transformation. It's been said that everybody

> *Everybody wants change, but few want to make that change happen.*

wants change, but few want to make that change happen. Many people who give their lives to Christ view their decision as a combining of their own lives with the best of what Jesus has to offer. You know, sort of like two companies merging into one in that win-win scenario. "Jesus, I am okay here, but I could use Your help over there." Such people desire a feel good faith that requires very little from them and a lot from God — of course only when they want His help.

This is a far cry from the clear conditions set forth by Jesus to be His follower, "If anyone desires to come after me, let him deny himself, and take up his cross, and follow me" (Matthew 16:24, NKJV). When you give your life to Christ you are not combining the best of your life with the best of His. NO! Instead you are being invited to die to yourself and give yourself completely to Him. To many this sounds quite strange and contrary to common sense. Jesus' teachings were often paradoxical. Do you want to save your life? Lose it! Do you want to be free? Become a slave! The irony is if you totally commit then the things you wanted all along will be yours.

Like David and Jonah, I believe your someday is here. You have a date with destiny. Doubt and fear are going to be driven out by faith and trust. Convenient 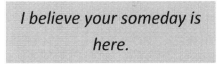 faith and conditional commitment will be replaced by steadfast belief and total dedication. For forty days we are going to a new level of sacrifice and obedience, a new level of dying to our own desires and allowing Him to live through us. Jesus said, "I have come that they may have life, and that they may have it more abundantly" (John 10:10, NKJV). The time has come to have that life right now.

The night before Jesus was crucified He faced His most difficult and emotionally draining time. Looking for companionship He asked His friends to be with Him in the Garden of Gethsemane. There He poured out His heart to His Father in prayer. When He returned to His disciples He found them sleeping. "'Couldn't you men keep watch with Me for one hour?' He asked Peter. 'Watch and pray so that you will not fall into temptation. The spirit is willing, but the flesh is weak'" (Matthew 26:40-41, NIV). Like the disciples, many of us are sleeping — sleeping giants. Down deep in our hearts we would like to live the abundant life. We sincerely want to honor God and experience the best He has for us but because we are flesh and blood we find it easy to fall prey to temptation. Jesus understands our fragile nature, which explains the challenge to stay awake and pray. I really like the Message paraphrase here, "There is a part of you that is eager, ready for anything in God. But there's another part that's as lazy as an old dog sleeping by the fire" (Matthew 26:41, MSG).

Who would you like to be in Christ? What would you do for the Lord if you knew you

Who would you like to be in Christ?

would not fail? What would you like to do on behalf of the Kingdom if you knew nothing could stop you? It's time to awaken the sleeping giant within and get back your cutting edge.

For those of you unsure I want to issue a challenge. Why not join us for Regenerate? You can view it as a forty-day test if you like. What do you have to lose? Worst case scenario it does not work for you. You have only lost forty days — slightly more than a month. Best case — your life is transformed forever. If this were an investment, I would call that a low risk — high reward opportunity of the highest caliber. In short, there is much to gain, little to lose.

Discussion Questions

1. Are you currently or have you ever danced around a "Goliath?" What do you believe held you back or is currently holding you back from confronting this giant?

2. "It's been said that everybody wants change, but few want to make that change happen." Do you agree with this statement? Why or why not? How have you personally experienced this in your life?

3. Who would you like to be in Christ? What would you do for the Lord if you knew you would not fail? What would you like to do on behalf of the Kingdom if you knew nothing could stop you?

CHAPTER TWO

Before And After

Before And After

*As a victim of a violent crime I was filled with anxiety, fear and panic attacks.
Doctors said I would always be mildly depressed. When I gave my life to Christ the
fear and anxiety began to lift and now there is so much joy in my life.*
- Debbie

Amazing before and after pictures popularized by exercise infomercials to provide surefire evidence of success make change look easy. Hard-bodied young men and women smile while exercising, as they seem to effortlessly lose fat and build muscle. Incredible muscle tone can be gained by a gadget small enough to fold up and put in your pocket. Dramatic weight loss is only a toll-free phone call away. And, of course, all this for only three easy payments. The message is clear — transformation is simple, convenient, easy and cheap! (I wonder if our churches and ministries do not sometimes fall into the same trap by offering quick and easy life solutions.)

Before and after pictures are all about potential — visual images of what we could look like, but don't. We can talk about potential forever because until it is developed potential it is just that — only talk. The thing about potential is that nothing has happened yet! "He had great potential," or "she never lived up to her potential," are sad comments about what might have been. For potential to be released it must be put in the right environment.

Lasting change and radical transformation is possible and available now. Regenerate is all about unleashing your

> *Regenerate is all about unleashing your potential.*

potential. But it is not without cost. You will have a few giants to face and bondages to break. In fact, your potential is hidden in your problems and obstacles. It took Goliath to release David's potential. The great fish that confined Jonah became his liberation. In other words, the same challenging issues that make change hard are the keys to transformation. As we preachers like to say, "No TESTimony without a test; no MESSage without a mess."

Of course there are always those who live in denial and do not have an accurate picture of themselves. Before and after pictures have no effect whatsoever. Why change when I'm fine as I am? My favorite part of American Idol is not seeing who makes it to the top ten and finally comes out on top, but the comical early episodes when some vocally challenged (and apparently delusional) people actually think they can win! Instead of being told by friends and family, "Yeah, dude, you should totally go for it," they need a Simon who will speak the painful truth, "Don't quit your day job." Confidence is great; overconfidence can be catastrophic. Dreams inspire; fantasies delude. One upside of life's problems, obstacles and difficult seasons is they can serve as a reality check. Maybe I'm not all that! Maybe I do need to change!

The Apostle Peter experienced a reality check that rocked his world. Peter was cocky and impetuous, confident

> *Good intentions and will power are not always enough.*

in his ability to succeed where others failed. Not that he was a bad guy. I believe his intentions were noble, coming from a pure heart. He really wanted to do what was right. But as we all know, good intentions and will power are not always enough. Peter would learn this the hard way.

As Jesus approached the end of His ministry He spoke to His disciples about the manner of His death and the fact that they would all fall away. Peter, who typically had something to say whether or not he had something to say, responded, "Even if all are made to stumble because of you, I will never be made to stumble" (Matthew 26:33, NKJV). He was adamant. He was sincere. He was passionate. But he was also wrong. Jesus looked Peter right in the eye and said, "Assuredly, I say to you that this night, before the rooster crows, you will deny me three times" (Matthew 26:34, NKJV). Still not convinced, Peter dared to disagree with his Lord concerning his will power, "Even if I have to die with you, I will not deny you" (Matthew 26:35, NKJV).

Peter's passion blinded him to some glaring weaknesses. He knew who he wanted to be and who he thought he was. He saw himself as loyal and committed, in this to the death. He genuinely loved Jesus and could not picture himself turning his back on his Lord. He knew he had what it takes.

Peter's strong will did take him where few dared to tread. When the guards came to arrest Jesus, he was ready to prove himself. Pulling out a sword he took a swipe at the head of the high priest's servant. The man must have ducked, or Peter had terrible aim, because he missed his head and ended up cutting off the man's ear. Jesus calmly rebuked Peter and then healed the man. (Evander Holyfield could have used Jesus in his corner a few years ago.) I think at that moment Peter would have died for Jesus. But circumstances did not go the way he thought they should go and from this point on things began to spiral out of control.

Making sure he was at a safe distance Peter followed Jesus to the courtyard outside the house where Jesus was being held.

"Now Peter was sitting out in the courtyard, and a servant girl came to him. 'You also were with Jesus of Galilee,' she said. But he denied it before them all. 'I don't know what you're talking about,' he said. Then he went out to the gateway, where another servant girl saw him and said to the people there, 'This fellow was with Jesus of Nazareth.' He denied it again, with an oath: 'I don't know the man!' After a little while, those standing there went up to Peter and said, 'Surely you are one of them; your accent gives you away.' Then he began to call down curses, and he swore to them, 'I don't know the man!' Immediately a rooster crowed. Then Peter remembered the word Jesus had spoken: 'Before the rooster crows, you will disown me three times.' And he went outside and wept bitterly" (Matthew 26:69-75, NIV).

Peter's world came crashing down. In one fell swoop he went from courageously fighting soldiers to cowardly denying to a little girl he even knew who Jesus was. Talk about up and down! He was

> *Will power had only taken him so far. He needed something more.*

now face to face with his own lack and brokenness and shame. He was not who he had imagined himself to be. Will power had only taken him so far. He needed something more.

Are you ever confused by your own ups and downs? One moment you are ready to charge hell with a water pistol, the next you cannot seem to stop yourself from doing the most stupid and self-destructive things. At times we think, *I can muscle through this situation. I can make my marriage work. I can figure out how to get my finances in order. I have what it takes to break free from this addiction. I can walk this Christian walk.* We really are being sincere; we are not playing games. But we quickly discover our sincere determination fails us at critical moments in our lives. As useful as will power can be, it is not always enough. How will we ever become who He has called us to be? How will we ever accomplish what we want to accomplish on behalf of the Kingdom? Like Peter, we need something more than will power.

Peter's regeneration, his total spiritual transformation, began on the morning of the resurrection. The women, who had arrived early on Sunday morning to prepare Jesus' body for burial, found not only an empty tomb but also an angel who instructed them. "Now go and tell his disciples, and especially Peter, that he will go ahead of you to Galilee. You will see him there, just as he told you" (Mark 16:7, CEV).

Why the special emphasis on Peter? How awkward was it going to be for Peter to see Jesus again face to face? Peter was ashamed of his cowardice and probably assumed Jesus was ashamed of him as well. What could he say? What would Jesus say to him? If accepted back in the family, he would surely need to go to the back of the line, a second class citizen. The special mention of Peter's name by the angel was, I believe, God's way of gently beginning the healing process in Peter. Peter needed to learn he was not merely forgiven, but still a person of destiny.

> *Peter needed to learn he was not merely forgiven, but still a person of destiny.*

Soon after Peter had an unexpected encounter with the resurrected Jesus that removed all doubts about God's stubborn love and full forgiveness. Having returned to his old way of handling life's pressures — fishing — Peter and his friends were wrapping up a frustrating day of abject failure. Not one fish! On the shore a man yelled out challenging them to throw their net on the other side of the vessel. The amazing result was a boatload of fish. Peter immediately recognized that this stunning turnaround had to be more than the consequence of good advice. It had to be a miracle. That was Jesus on the shore!

No longer bound by fear and shame, Peter jumped out of the boat and swam to shore. Swimming toward Jesus in faith rather than running away from Him in shame proved to be life-changing. Moments later the others arrived with a boat full of fish and a wonderful meal was had by all. But that is not the end of Peter's story of transformation.

"When they had finished eating, Jesus said to Simon Peter, 'Simon son of John, do you love me more than these?' 'Yes, Lord,' he said, 'you know that I love you.' Jesus said, 'Feed my lambs'" (John 21:15, NIV).

Jesus was not simply asking Peter if he loved Him more than fish sticks. He was asking Peter if he loved Him more than his old life — his former way of making a living, having fun, and coping with life's pressures. When Peter said, "Yes," Jesus gave him a new assignment — "feed my lambs." But Jesus was not done.

"Again Jesus said, 'Simon son of John, do you love me?' He answered, 'Yes, Lord, you know that I love you.' Jesus said, 'Take care of my sheep'" (John 21:16, NIV).

Repetition emphasizes the critical nature of the discussion. Breaking news — Jesus *already* knew Peter loved Him. He had *already* forgiven Peter. This discourse is not giving Jesus previously unknown information, rather it is leading Peter to accept the realities of the past and discover the potential of the future. The real question was could Peter forgive himself. Could Peter move beyond the disappointments and failures of his past in order to embrace the new assignment of the future?

Like Peter, we are sometimes so overwhelmed by the guilt and shame of our past that we miss God's love and forgiveness and therefore hope for the future. A happily remarried ex reminds you of the lingering consequences of past infidelities. A prosperous former business partner takes you back to what could have been if only you had not acted so foolishly. Like spilled milk, some things cannot be recovered. Still, God's mercy offers forgiveness and His grace provides fresh beginnings. Old dreams may be forever dashed, but God offers new assignments.

> *Old dreams may be forever dashed, but God offers new assignments.*

"The third time he said to him, 'Simon son of John, do you love me?' Peter was hurt because Jesus asked him the third time, 'Do you love me?' He said, 'Lord, you know all things; you know that I love you.' Jesus said, 'Feed my sheep'" (John 21:17, NIV).

Peter was bothered and a little upset the third time Jesus asked him the same basic question. Again, the questioning was not for the Lord's benefit but Peter's. Jesus did not need to be convinced of Peter's love for Him after embarrassing denials, but Peter needed clarity in his own mind. His new life mission would forever change the world, but it would come with great personal sacrifice. It would eventually cost him his life.

"'Very truly I tell you, when you were younger you dressed yourself and went where you wanted; but when you are old you will stretch out your hands, and someone else will dress you and lead you where you do not want to go.' Jesus said this to indicate the kind of death by which Peter would glorify God. Then he said to him, 'Follow me'" (John 21:18-19, NIV)!

Peter would indeed follow Jesus. He had encountered the resurrected Lord and was forever changed. Per the instruction of Jesus, Peter waited for the outpouring of the Holy Spirit. No longer was he depending on will power. His life was regenerated. Within just a few short weeks after his embarrassing denial in front of a little girl he preached a bold message resulting in thousands of people giving their lives to Christ. He became a foundational figure in establishing and leading the early church when it turned the world upside down. When his mission was complete, early Christian sources tells us Peter died heroically. Like his Lord, he was crucified. Unlike Jesus, he was crucified upside down at his own request, as he did not feel worthy to die in the same manner as his Lord.

Talk about a before and after picture! This is radical transformation. What changes someone like that? What will change you? Not will power alone. Peter needed resurrection power. What if you could experience this resurrection power as a present reality in your life? Regenerate moves you from will power to resurrection power. A new you in forty days!

Discussion Questions

1. How would you describe your current "before" picture? How different might your "after" picture look?

2. Does your past (the good, the bad and the ugly) have a grip on you? What do you need to let go of? How might you need to embrace forgiveness and grace?

3. How does (or would) clarifying your own love for Christ and your commitment to Him support you in living out God's purpose for your life?

4. Will power alone will not transform your life. You need resurrection power. Are you ready for resurrection power to become a present reality in your life?

CHAPTER THREE

Forty Days

Forty Days

My wife gave up TV and I gave up booze. I don't watch TV now to support her, we end up spending time with our kids or reading the Bible. God is even blessing us with a home – we're in escrow now. This Regenerate thing is working faster than I ever imagined!
- Travis

Forty days. Why forty? It's just a number. Forty days is only a little more than a month. Not too long. When I was a child and my mom told me to go to my room for ten minutes every second ticked by painfully slow. Forty minutes? Forget about it — might as well be forever! Now forty days can pass in the blink of an eye. It's been said life is short — it goes by quickly. Marguerite and I have been married for forty years. It does not seem possible. We still feel like kids. Where did the time go? On the other hand, life is long. Forty minutes can come to a virtual standstill while sweating on an exercise machine. Forty years is a long time to stay faithful to one's spouse, a long time to maintain one's integrity. Marguerite and I may feel like kids, but the reality is we now have grandkids. I guess life is short, but at the same time it is also long. The same can be true of forty days.

The number forty has been in people's conscience in recent times due in part to Rick Warren's best seller, *Forty Days of Purpose*. The idea of radical change taking place during a forty-day period is not new however. In the Bible the number forty represents radical change and transformation.

- It rained for forty days and nights when God cleansed the world and prepared for new beginnings.
- Moses was on the mountain with God for forty days and his face shone with glory for another forty days as he was transformed.
- Twelve spies spent forty days spying out the better life God had for them in the Promised Land.
- Israel spent forty years in the wilderness being readied to enter that Promised Land.
- The giant Goliath arrogantly challenged Israel for forty days before falling to David.
- A fearful and depressed Elijah spent forty days on Mount Horeb before the Lord passed by and spoke to him.
- The people of Nineveh repented and experienced deliverance after hearing Jonah preach for forty days.
- Jesus fasted for forty days before defeating the devil and launching His ministry.
- The resurrected Jesus appeared on earth for forty days before ascending to heaven.

It is apparent that when talking about real and lasting change the number forty is significant. It represents a period of testing and trial preparing us for breakthrough and next level living.

I remember when the Lord first started speaking to me about Regenerate my first thought was it sounded a lot like

Lent — not that I knew very much about the subject. Growing up some of my best friends were Roman Catholic. One day at school they would show up with dirty foreheads and tell me they could not have dessert for a while. I learned they were supposed to give up something they loved, like chocolate or cussing or whatever, though at the time I was not sure why. Over the years I discovered that the season of Lent covered forty days, excluding Sundays. Lent begins with Ash Wednesday (that was not dirt after all!) and leads up to Easter, though for most Catholics it ends on Holy Thursday.

As I looked into Lent I discovered it was about more than giving up dessert. Lent is intended to be a time of fasting (from foods and festivities), sacrifice and penance. It is a time to seek the Lord and draw closer to Him. For many, however, Lent has little to do with God. Some of the world's most notorious and decadent parties originated as

> *It is a time to seek the Lord and draw closer to Him.*

a Christian's last chance for excess before Lent begins. Rio de Janeiro's *Carnival* and New Orleans' *Mardi Gras* are prime examples. Those events may be a lot of things, but they certainly do not in any way, shape or form represent those who have a heart for God. It is like bingeing before dieting, going on a bender before going to AA, hitting the mall on a spending spree before declaring bankruptcy. The prophets were never shy about slamming God's people for turning holy festivals into excuses for indulging the flesh and ignoring Him. Still, I was touched by the original good intention of setting aside time to get oneself ready for Easter and resurrection. That sounded like a great idea.

I also wondered when God first spoke to me about Regenerate if it were another fasting experience. Some of my friends and acquaintances in the ministry lead very effective fasting campaigns. Or perhaps it was a prayer thing. My life had been transformed years ago by studying and daily praying the Lord's Prayer. I even wondered if Regenerate was supposed to be yet another fund raising crusade. Or, if not merely about finances, maybe Regenerate was about the giving of time and talent.

As I pondered these questions in my heart things began to come increasingly into focus. Is Regenerate a renewed form of Lent? In some ways. It is about seriously seeking the Lord in anticipation of honoring His resurrection and experiencing our own renewal. Is it a prayer thing? Absolutely, and more. Is it a fasting thing? Yes, but it involves so much more. Is it a giving thing? Definitely, and more. Regenerate is a forty-day journey of pursuing God, self-inventory and the exercise of spiritual disciplines resulting in dynamic spiritual empowerment. It is a time to reflect. It is a time to draw near. It is a time to grow.

It is a time to reflect.
It is a time to draw near.
It is a time to grow.

You may be tempted to think you do not have the time — even forty days. We live in a fast paced culture filled with traffic, stress, crowds and noise. We cry out to God to speak to us or give us a sign but often our world is so loud and cluttered we either cannot hear Him or are distracted. Taking the time to pursue God is an investment rather than expenditure. In other words, sacrificing a little of our time now will pay off later. If your plate is already full, take some things off your plate, at least for the next forty days, and see what God can do. During Regenerate we are going to slow down, turn down the noise and cut out the distractions. In the words of the Psalmist, "Be still, and know that I am God" (Psalm 46:10, NIV).

Abraham had to step out of his comfort zone when visited by the Lord. Sure, the desert sun was hot and the shade of his tent provided relief, but when Abraham saw the three angelic guests he jumped up and ran to meet them. He sensed it was a unique opportunity not to be missed. His reward? God confirmed Abraham's destiny (Genesis 18). Are you willing to jump at this opportunity? By stepping out of life as usual we allow God to breathe new life and purpose into us.

What exactly then is the Lord asking of us for Regenerate? If it is similar but not quite the same as Lent, fasting, praying, or giving for forty days, what are we supposed to do? Specifically, we are asking for three things.

Give Up

What are you willing to give up for the Lord during these forty days? It might be something you love like desserts, television or, dare I say it — shopping (Marguerite) or golf (Jim). Remember that whatever you decide to give up needs to be something that means a lot to you. For example, I cannot stand asparagus. I think it is demonic.

Marguerite thinks it is heavenly. It would be no problem for me not to eat asparagus for forty days, or the rest of my life for that matter, but obviously it would not really involve giving up anything.

It could be concentrating on giving up a bad or destructive habit like smoking cigarettes or, more seriously, drugs. Who knows? Maybe a concerted forty-day effort could lead to long-term victory. At any rate, we are not intending to look spiritual or to earn brownie points with God. A key here is to remember you are giving this up for the Lord and can use this time for constructive purposes as you pursue Him. Which leads us to the next point.

Start Up

What good thing have you been putting off? What healthy habit do you need to start? It could be reading your Bible regularly, working out, serving at church, eating more healthy food, any one of a myriad of things. Starting up can be a real key to sustainable giving up. It has long been known that it is difficult to stop destructive habits without replacing them with healthy habits — the replacement principle. And remember, we are not asking at this point for a life commitment, just for a forty-day "experiment," if you will. Obviously we are hoping and praying for lasting change, but there are times it is helpful to start simple. How do you eat an elephant? One bite at a time.

Step Up

Transformation does not happen simply by focusing on ourselves and our own needs and problems. It is important to help others. What are some practical ways you can step up and sacrificially give of your *time*, *talent* and *treasure*? Do not sit back and wait for others to do it. Do not think that what you have to offer is not large enough, good enough, or important enough. It is. And giving is just as important for you as for the people or causes you may be helping.

Notice too that to really step up means to give sacrificially. Many have given liberally and generously without ever giving sacrificially. A true sacrifice is something valuable, something that you need; it is not something you can afford to give away. If that is the case, why would anyone ever sacrificially give something of value?

> *A true sacrifice is something valuable, something that you need.*

People will only give sacrificially when they perceive the person or cause they are giving to is of greater value. Soldiers have sacrificially given their very lives because they loved their friends, family and nation. To such heroes some things are more important than life itself. King David turned down an offer from a wealthy man that would have provided what he needed to sacrifice to the Lord while away from home. Why? His answer is clear, "No, I insist on paying the full price. I will not take for the LORD what is yours, or sacrifice a burnt offering that costs me nothing" (1 Chronicles 21:24, NIV).

Give up. Start up. Step up. The time to start is now.

Growing up many of us played the game *Red Light, Green Light*. The words "green light" signaled you were allowed to race toward the finish line, but as soon as the words "red light" were spoken you had to come to a sudden halt. If you failed to stop you had to go back to the beginning and start over. The goal of the person calling out "red light, green light" seemed to be to

God wants us to win!

get you to fail. Not so with God's directions. He has plans to prosper and not to harm us, to give us hope and a future (see Jeremiah 29:11). God wants us to win! Let's apply this game to Regenerate and, for good measure, add a yellow light like we find with traffic signals.

Red means stop! Are you sensing God telling you to stop something in your life right now? God is not a cosmic killjoy — He is not trying to bug you but to bless you. When God asks you to give up something, good or bad, it is with the intention of bringing something better into your life. Sin, for example, is often fun in the short run but destructive in the long run. This is why when it comes to a real game, the race of life, the author of Hebrews instructs us to "...throw off everything that hinders and the sin that so easily entangles" (Hebrews 12:1, NIV).

We continue at our own peril when we ignore God's red light. How dangerous it would be if we all just drove through the intersection whenever we felt like it ignoring the signs and signals. Penalties come with running a red light. Injury and death can be the result of ignoring traffic signals. We know that. Yet, in our personal lives we believe we know more than the Signal Maker. We think, *Oh I know I should stop*, but we do not. We must remember we do not control the signal, God does and we ignore or disobey at our own risk. God's signal is always for our good.

Yellow means slow down! Proceed with caution. Some see a yellow light and do the exact opposite — they speed up in order to try to beat the light so they do not have to wait. We live in a culture that wants, and often expects, instant gratification. We want it all and we want it now. This can lead to a thoughtless impatience that leads to reckless decisions.

God's yellow light is not a red light, that is to say it is not necessarily a divine "no," but it is a clear sign to slow down. It might be a dating relationship, a business venture, a hobby, or a large purchase. Whatever it is may not be a bad thing in and of itself, but

> *God may be telling you to slow down until the timing is right and it is safe for you to proceed.*

it may be growing into a higher priority than God. Are you pushing for something or rushing into something whose time has not yet come? God may be telling you to slow down until the timing is right and it is safe for you to proceed.

Waiting is seldom easy or fun, but the results are typically better than anticipated. "But those who wait on the LORD shall renew their strength; they shall mount up with wings like eagles, they shall run and not be weary, they shall walk and not faint" (Isaiah 40:31, NKJV).

Green means go! We have all been behind someone who for whatever reason fails to move when the green light appears. What's going on? What's the problem? At first we try patiently waiting under the assumption movement is imminent. But no! They just stay parked at the light. "It ain't gonna get any greener," we think (or shout!). If the crew in the apparently parked car do not look like escaped convicts, we may finally resort to beeping our horn.

I wonder if at times the Holy Spirit feels the same way with us. We ask God for opportunities and breakthrough in our lives, yet when God in His time provides an obvious open door we freeze. We may hear the voice of the Lord saying, "Go!" He may even honk at us through our spouse, children, boss and maybe even our dog. It is time to go for it. It is time to step out. It is time to trust God and follow Him.

It is time to trust God and follow Him.

It is far easier to be a fan of Jesus than a follower of Jesus. Fans get to sit on the sideline cheering the participants on. Followers are on the field actively engaged in the game. Jesus did not come to organize a fan club, He came to build a church. Jesus declared no opponent, not even the very gates of Hades, would prevail against His church. It is alive and vibrant and relevant. And it is filled with followers.

The time has come to get out of the stands and join the team on the field. The team is not complete without you — and you may never be complete without the team. The game is not that long — only forty days — but by giving up, starting up and stepping up you will experience transformation that will last a lifetime.

Discussion Questions

1. "We live in a fast paced culture filled with traffic, stress, crowds and noise. We cry out to God to speak to us or give us a sign but often our world is so loud and cluttered we either cannot hear Him or are distracted." Can you relate to this? What is it that makes your life loud and cluttered?

2. What might you be able to take off your plate for the next 40 days to enable you to hear God more clearly?

3. What will you give up, start up and step up during Regenerate?

4. In the past, when God gave you a red light, yellow light or green light how did you respond to it? Which color light is the most difficult for you to obey? What color is the light He is giving you now?

CHAPTER FOUR

Power Of Pursuit

Power Of Pursuit

In the height of my addiction I was living on the streets going from drug house to drug house. I ended up in jail where I saw Pastor Jim on Balanced Living TV. Upon my release I began attending the 12-step program at Faith. I now chase God like I used to chase drugs. God saved my life.
- Darryll

The heart of Regenerate is setting aside forty days to focus on pursuing God. Great reward is promised to those who move beyond typical casual inspection to aggressive pursuit. Check out what Jesus said, "But seek first the kingdom of God and his righteousness, and all these things shall be added unto you" (Matthew 6:33, NKJV). Can you take forty days to put God first and see what happens? "But without faith it is impossible to please him, for he who comes to God must believe that he is, and that he is a rewarder of those who diligently seek him" (Hebrews 11:6, NKJV). Can you trust God for forty days to reward you with blessings greater than the thrills you may be giving up as you seek Him? Pursuing God diligently for forty days will bring some of the greatest blessings ever experienced and breakthroughs desired for years.

> *Can you take forty days to put God first and see what happens?*

Are we then trying to earn our blessings by being good boys and girls for forty days? Are we trying to manipulate God? Are we viewing the Lord as a slightly more sophisticated version of Santa Claus? No, we are simply taking seriously the promises of a Father who is eager, as is any parent who loves their children, to bless His kids. Love gives, love lavishes and love blesses. But if we, as the objects of God's love, put ourselves outside His sphere, His Kingdom, we are in no position to receive. We must place ourselves, as the old time Pentecostals were apt to say, "under the spout where the glory comes out."

While repentance, prayer, fasting and seeking the Lord should be the ongoing practice of every believer, it frequently is not. Note that in the most famous sermon ever preached, Jesus said not *if*, but *when* you give (Matthew 6:2); not *if*, but *when* you pray (Matthew 6:5); and not *if*, but *when* you fast (Matthew 6:16). Regenerate gives us a great opportunity to introduce, or perhaps reintroduce, these spiritual disciplines into our Christian walk. For those already practicing these disciplines, Regenerate provides a season of intensification, not unlike putting your car into turbo or your space vehicle into warp speed.

When all is said and done, Regenerate is not so much about praying, fasting, and giving. It is not focused on the stuff we give up, start up and step up. Rather it is all about doing anything and everything to know Him, to serve Him and to love Him.

Jesus compared the Kingdom to a treasure in a field. "The kingdom of heaven is like treasure hidden in a field. When a man found it, he hid it again, and then in his joy went and sold all he had and bought the field" (Matthew 13:44, NIV). This man did not sacrifice everything because the field was a fantastic piece of real estate. It was neither beachfront property nor located in a beautiful mountain resort. They say it's what's inside that counts. That was certainly the case for this lucky man. Like a fortune seeker in the California gold rush days, he knew "there's gold in them there hills!"

What price are you willing to pay for the field? What are you willing to sacrifice? Regenerate is a short season of sacrifice with long-term results. Within this field of forty days lies your treasure.

> *Regenerate is a short season of sacrifice with long-term results.*

By using "treasure" as a word picture of the Kingdom Jesus was connecting with a world consumed with the pursuit of material wealth. Can anything really be more important than fame, fun and fortune? Is there more to life than power, pleasure and prestige? The truth is people who would never consider sacrificing anything to pursue God will do whatever it takes in their own pursuit of "the girls, the gold and the glory." While critical of "religious fanatics" they are often fanatical in their own chase of the endorphin rush stemming from drugs, sexual experimentation and criminal activity.

Others find an equally addictive buzz in the pursuit of more legitimate endeavors such as making a name for themselves in the sports or entertainment industries or achieving a lifestyle of the rich and famous in the world of business and finance. Many families sacrificially adjust their entire schedules around travel ball teams, dance competitions and the like. Who cannot admire the sacrifice many parents make, often working long, hard hours so the kids can go to college and make a better life? Whether legit or illegitimate, noble or selfish, we all know what it means to seriously pursue something. Why can't we do the same for God?

> *We all know what it means to seriously pursue something. Why can't we do the same for God?*

Moses is listed in the Hall of Fame of Faith not because of what he had attained, rather because of the sacrificial choices he made to pursue God. Moses was almost killed as an infant for no other crime than being born a Jew, but a desperate though faith-filled act by his mother resulted in his being rescued by the daughter of Pharaoh. Consequently, he was privileged to be raised in the wealthiest and most powerful household on the planet. Talk about "lucking out" — Moses was the original fresh prince of Bel Air (okay, Cairo). By the time he was a young man he had everything a typical red-blooded American male could possibly want. At his fingertips were political power, educational opportunities and business prospects. If he had wanted to be lazy, he could have passed the days lying on a hammock by the Nile being fanned and hand fed grapes by beer commercial quality looking women. For Moses, however, the choices were clear.

"By faith Moses, when he had grown up, refused to be known as the son of Pharaoh's daughter. He chose to be mistreated along with the people of God rather than to enjoy the fleeting pleasures of sin. He regarded disgrace for the sake of Christ as of greater value than the treasures of Egypt, because he was looking ahead to his reward" (Hebrews 11:24-26, NIV).

When Moses finally grew up (everyone grows old; not everyone grows up), he settled the identity crisis — he was a child of God not simply a rich celebrity. That meant taking responsibility and making the tough choices rather than enjoying the perks of fame and fortune. He had discovered personal power, pleasure and prestige came with a catch — their pleasures were fleeting and not ultimately satisfying. To walk with God was way more valuable than to "walk like an Egyptian." He found the treasure in the field.

One of the famous saints of church history, Augustine, was born of a pagan father and Christian mother. As a youth Augustine followed in his father's footsteps and was quite the wealthy playboy. His mother, however, refused to give up and eventually her prayers prevailed as he came to Christ. However, his lustful lifestyle did not magically disappear. Augustine later confessed to one of the more famous and amusing prayers of all time, "Grant me chastity and continence, only not yet." For those not fluent in archaic English, let me translate, "God, deliver me from lust — but not yet!" Some of you might be able to relate to his honesty. Like Moses, Augustine eventually grew up and chose to pursue God. Not convinced he had really changed, his favorite mistress ran into him and could not believe he was ignoring her. She got right in his face and said, "Augustine, it is I." He simply replied, "But it is not I," and kept walking. Augustine was not the same anymore. He was a new person. He had found the treasure in the field and, forsaking all else, pursued it with all his heart. He had been regenerated.

Whatever we have to let go of in our pursuit of God He will replace with something far better — beauty for ashes, joy for mourning, praise for depression, love for lust, light for darkness, hope for despair. But this level of pursuit involves more than simply "checking out this religious thing." Remember Cheech and Chong's parody of Jesus Freaks? "I used to be all messed up on drugs. Then I found Jesus. Now I'm all messed up on Jesus." But Jesus is not simply another trip. He is the one and only Son of God who rescued us from the dominion of darkness and set us free. So pursuing God means we move from simply checking out God to actively seeking out God. God is asking us to grow up, decide who we are, and pursue Him with all our hearts.

One powerful effect of pursuing God is the restoration of the proper connections that make life work. The older I get the more I see the wisdom in the old adage, "It's not what you know but who you know." It is all about our connections. People, like cell phones and household appliances, do not work without connection. Is it not frustrating to be on the verge of closing that important deal when the phone loses reception? Or how about those times we talk on and on before realizing the person on the other end has not been there for most of our brilliant discourse. Can you hear me now? You still there? I remember almost losing my salvation in anger over a television that was not working during an important ballgame (what will the Lakers do if I cannot watch?) only to have my wife discover it had become unplugged (ah, must have been the grandkids). It should have been the first thing I checked. When life is not working, the first thing we should do is check our connections. Are we plugged in?

The three spiritual disciplines discussed by Jesus in the Sermon on the Mount — prayer, fasting and giving — deal with key spiritual connections. First, *prayer* connects us with *God*. As stated earlier, success in life is often the result of who we know rather than what we know. Talk about knowing the right person! Prayer is our direct line to God. Many view prayer as a hotline only to be used in case of dire emergency. To the contrary, prayer is the main power source from which everything else flows. In other words,

> *Prayer is the main power source from which everything else flows.*

we can and should do other things than pray, but we should do nothing without prayer. Prayer is more than asking God to meet our needs and grant our desires; it is, along with the Word, a primary way of getting to know Him. Paul writes, "I keep asking that the God of our Lord Jesus Christ, the glorious Father, may give you the Spirit of wisdom and revelation, so that you may know him better. I pray the eyes of your heart may be enlightened in order that you may know the hope to which he has called you, the riches of his glorious inheritance in his holy people" (Ephesians 1:17-18, NIV).

Fasting connects us with *ourselves*. Fasting focuses on the real us — not our outside but our inside. We are so accustomed to doing whatever our bodies and minds tell us that it is a shock to the system when their demands are not immediately met. Typically if we are hungry, we eat; if sleepy, we sleep. Schedules may determine how soon we are able to fulfill these needs, but we do not put them off for long. Fasting reminds us that a Greater Force now operates in our lives.

The Bible says we are made up of body, soul and spirit. Before we come to Christ our body and soul reign while our spirit lies dormant. When we are born again our spirit comes alive and the Holy Spirit takes the reins as our spirit is revived. Now the old order of body-soul-spirit begins to be reversed. As we grow in the Lord the new order becomes spirit-soul-body. Old patterns of living are replaced with new priorities. Fasting lets our body know that just because it wants something does not mean it is going to get it; it is not in charge anymore. Fasting does the same with our mind. We are no longer limited or dominated by our body and soul.

> *Sometimes the final touches of our own healing waits until we get out of God's hospital bed to help someone else.*

Giving connects us with *others*. It is all too easy to become self-absorbed even when doing something seemingly as spiritual as pursuing God. The Great Commandment does tell us to love the Lord with all our heart, soul, mind and strength, but the second half reminds us to "love your neighbor as yourself." At the risk of sounding like a cliché we are blessed to be a blessing. In fact, sometimes the final touches of our own healing waits until we get out of God's hospital bed to help someone else. You just may be somebody else's answer to prayer.

When we pursue God and are connected by prayer, fasting and giving our lives become focused. And a focused life is a powerful life. Consider a laser. A laser is essentially light amplified and intensely focused. Light illuminates a room. Focused light, however, can play music on a cd or perform a delicate surgical procedure. Powerful and focused light can even cut through steel. Focus brings intensification.

One of the most frustrating things in ministry is preaching to people week after week, month after month, year after year, who have nuclear potential but who settle for firecracker lives. Like light transforming into a laser beam, the forty days of Regenerate can turn firecrackers into weapons of mass destruction aimed at the powers of darkness, bondage and addiction. As we focus on prayer, fasting and giving our glancing is transformed into gazing. Many spend most of their time *gazing* at life's problems and opportunities and only occasionally *glancing* at God. That glance may be restricted to a few moments on Sunday morning at church or perhaps pausing while channel surfing to watch a few minutes of Christian television. Regenerate reverses that as we spend more time gazing at the Lord and merely glancing at our problems. God's Word says, "fixing our eyes on Jesus, the pioneer and perfecter of faith"

(Hebrews 12:2, NIV). As the Old Testament prophets simply put it, "It is time to seek the Lord!"

Discussion Questions

1. "Whatever we have to let go of in our pursuit of God He will replace with something far better — beauty for ashes, joy for mourning, praise for depression, love for lust, light for darkness, hope for despair." How have you experienced this in the past?

2. Prayer connects us with God, fasting connects us with ourselves and giving connects us with others. How are your connections?

3. What would it look like for you to passionately pursue God?

CHAPTER FIVE

Discipline Leads To Freedom

Discipline Leads To Freedom

Growing up my home life was abusive and chaotic.
In my search for a family I joined a gang. My life soon hit rock bottom and I decided
to visit Faith where I gave my life to Christ. Pastor Jim told me that the church was
now my family. I am so happy. I am married, have a great job and am doing
something great with my life by serving God.
- Jorge

I have a confession to make. I do not enjoy going to the gym to exercise. I seldom look forward to it. I do not enjoy the experience of working out while I am at the club. The treadmill, the lifecycle, lifting weights — these are things I at best tolerate. So why do I pay for gym privileges? Years ago Marguerite bought me a lifetime membership to a local health club. For the first couple of years I did not go once. I figured there was no need to rush — I had a whole lifetime. Around the same time I remember sitting in bed and eating donuts while watching Denise Austin host a work out show on television. I can still hear her encouraging words, "You're doing great! You're doing great!" I was supposed to be exercising along with her, but I was simply watching her exercise. I was not doing great! I was eating a donut in bed!

Watching somebody else exercise apparently has little to no benefit. Who knew? I finally made the choice to go to the gym and give exercise a try. My motivation was neither noble nor healthy. I figured if I worked out I could eat whatever I wanted and not gain weight. For example, I love warm pecan pie with ice cream. Since I do not like the ice cream to melt and make a mess all over my plate, I tend to eat the entire dessert within a few minutes. One day I made the mistake of seeing how many calories are in a typical piece of pecan pie a la mode — what do you think? I was shocked to see, depending on the size, it is in the 800 to 1200 range. When I first began to go to the gym I could not help but notice how slowly calories are burned even with intense exercise. Do you know how long it takes to burn 800 – 1200 calories on a StairMaster or treadmill? Forever! In fact if you are ever told you have only five minutes to live and want to make it last as long as possible, get on a StairMaster. The seconds and calories slowly tick by. It does not seem fair! It only takes a few minutes to easily consume an enormous amount of calories, on the other hand it takes a lot of vigorous work and hard time to burn a few.

My lifetime membership ended when the health club went out of business. At that point I had to make a decision if I was willing to pay for something I had been getting for free (via my wife's gift). However, in the previous few years my motive for working out had changed. Although exercising was still not particularly fun, I did like how it made me feel. I had more energy, and I just plain old felt better physically, emotionally and even spiritually. I noticed a major positive difference between the weeks I exercised and the weeks I did not.

Like exercise, the word discipline conjures up negative images in the minds of many. Discipline sounds hard, boring and sometimes impossible. "I'm just not disciplined" is a comment I frequently hear. Happily, however, again like exercise discipline has surprising rewards.

Spiritual Discipline Is Liberating

Who would think if you are tired that exercise, along with proper rest, might be the cure? But the expenditure of energy in exercise ends up bringing more energy. Who would think the needed restrictions necessitated by practicing discipline actually lead to freedom and liberty? But restricting how much television we watch, or how much time we spend social networking, or playing video games in order to pray, read the Word, and serve others will lead to more fun, more time and more personal freedom. In short, discipline leads to liberty.

If you are one of those who feels you have a full plate — you are convinced you literally cannot add one more thing to your schedule — my advice would be to wisely experiment with taking a few things off your plate for forty days. If you are too busy for God, you are too busy. You might discover that some of those things you thought you could not live without are not so essential after all. The new freedom and joy arising from your spiritual exercise will speak for themselves.

If you are too busy for God, you are too busy.

The hardest part of any exercise program is getting started. Even once the decision is made to begin it is easy to immediately give up thinking, "It's too hard!" However, if we simply hang in there and get over the initial hump things begin to get easier.

One of the best days of my life was when I turned sixteen, passed my driver's test and received my license. I felt like Dr. King — free at last! I lacked one critical thing, however — a car. Having no money I was quite excited that my grandad gave me his old car. Cannot complain about free, but the car was more of a slow boat than an automobile (which in hindsight I am sure my parents were happy about). The 1960 Ford was bare bones having no carpet or radio. It's huge body and tiny engine were capable of accelerating from zero to sixty in about four minutes. You had to be a muscle builder just to roll up the windows (Hey kids, car windows were not always powered with a simple switch). The foot pedal clutch was difficult to push down, but not as difficult as working the gearshift located on the steering wheel column. And talk about steering, this was before the day and age of power steering so the car was very difficult to turn, especially if you were driving slowly and shifting gears at the same time. Between rolling up the window, pushing in the clutch, shifting the gear and trying to turn the car around a corner you had your P90X workout right there. On top of all this, I was a new driver trying to remember all the rules of driving and checking all my mirrors. Only my desire for my new found "independence" kept me from giving up.

I distinctly recall feeling overwhelmed when I first became a father. I was so excited the day Marguerite and I brought our first child Dan home from the hospital. That first night we cautiously placed him in a bassinet in our bedroom. All night long if he made the slightest noise I jumped up with concern. The next morning I was exhausted from the excitement and lack of sleep. Human beings had obviously survived being parents for thousands of years, yet I remember thinking after just one night of parenthood, "I can't do this!"

Before Marguerite and I were married she was hired by a local grocery store to be a checker. Before scanners checkers had to manually push in the price of an item and memorize codes for all the various fruit and vegetables. Marguerite is bright — she has a high IQ, and did phenomenal in school. Still, learning all these codes drove her nuts. Even on dates I could not help but notice she was not really present. Her mind was full of prices and codes. Even for a woman with a knack for math, the codes and numbers seemed overwhelming.

Well, as you might guess, the skills needed to drive a difficult stick shift car became rather routine. Parenting is never easy, but I survived those first few days and am now a proud grandpa. The codes and numbers became so easy for Marguerite that eventually she could carry on a conversation, or plan a delicious dinner, while checking groceries at the store. With a little effort and persistence, things that once seemed impossible and overwhelming become quite doable, even routine.

Do not be intimidated at the prospect of starting up or renewing some healthy spiritual disciplines. You can do it! Over time these disciplines will become second nature and bring liberation in areas where you currently are not free. "If you stick with this, living out what I tell you, you are my disciples for sure. Then you will experience for yourselves the truth, and the truth will free you" (John 8:32, MSG).

Another way of looking at this is what I call the four D's: desire, decision, discipline and delight. Everything starts with desire. You will never passionately pursue something you do not want, no matter how much your mother or spouse want it for you. Desire alone, however, is not enough. A decision must be made to actually do something. Decision turns wanting into doing. You decide to move beyond wanting to read your Bible to actually starting to read it. You start praying. You start giving. You start exercising. You start dieting.

Moving from desire to decision is not sufficient. Discipline is the requisite next step. Discipline turns a nice start into a healthy habit. For those able to navigate from desire to decision to discipline a wonderful reward awaits — delight. I like to call it the "hallelujah side of obedience." Before the days of automated ski lifts the pioneers of downhill skiing had to trudge up a steep, snowy, and sometimes slippery mountainside with crude wooden skis strapped on their backs. Why all the effort? For the thrill of the downhill run. On the other side of your efforts awaits the thrill of breakthrough and liberation. Your "hallelujah side" is waiting.

> *On the other side of your efforts awaits the thrill of breakthrough and liberation.*

Spiritual Discipline Is Life Giving

"'For I know the plans I have for you,' declares the Lord, 'plans to prosper you and not to harm you, plans to give you hope and a future'" (Jeremiah 29:11, NIV). Do you believe this? Every principle God gives His children is not merely good advice, it is life-giving. At some point we all have to decide if God's way is

> *At some point we all have to decide if God's way is better than any other.*

better than any other. Once convinced, it makes sense to follow His directions.

The world's plans typically promise more than they can deliver. One of my favorite episodes of the original Twilight Zone series is called "A Nice Place to Visit." It is about a small town crook who wakes up in eternity after being killed in a shoot-out with the police. He is met by a personal guide who ensures he is given everything he desires but never had during life on earth. He is provided with a penthouse, beautiful women, plenty of cash and unlimited luck in gambling. He has a hard time believing a petty thief like him made it to heaven. Soon, however, despite now having everything he had always wanted, boredom and dissatisfaction set in. In his frustration he asks his angel to send him to the "other place," thinking he must not be the right fit for heaven. At that request, the guide laughs. With the sound of his laughter growing from angelic to demonic, he declares, "This IS the other place!" In closing we hear narrator Rod Serling's haunting words: "A scared, angry little man who never got a break. Now he has everything he's ever wanted — and he's going to have to live with it for eternity in the Twilight Zone."

Be careful what you wish for. God's blessings, to the contrary, are everything they are cracked up to be and they do not come with a hangover — or regret — or bondage. "The blessing of the Lord makes one rich, and he adds no sorrow with it" (Proverbs 10:22, NKJV). If you are far from God and suffering the consequences of bad life choices, running to God rather than away from Him is the answer. "'Even now,' declares the LORD, 'return to me with all your heart, with fasting and weeping and mourning. …I will repay you for the years the locusts have eaten…'" (Joel 2:12, 25, NIV). Not only is it never too late for God, things and circumstances are never too far-gone for Him. Even now God can turn things around in your life. The effects of wasted days and wasted nights (sorry Freddie Fender), perhaps wasted decades, can be reversed EVEN NOW! It is *always* too soon to quit and failure is *never final*.

> *It is always too soon to quit and failure is never final.*

Spiritual Discipline Is Empowering

We opened this chapter noting how I do not enjoy going to the gym. Still, I go several times a week because working out empowers me in a way other endeavors I do enjoy, like golf, do not. I am empowered physically with increased strength, endurance and energy. I am empowered mentally with greater alertness and clarity of thought. I am empowered emotionally as I feel less stressed and more balanced. The benefits make the effort well worth it. Paul sees spiritual exercise as even more beneficial. "...train yourself to be godly. For physical training is of some value, but godliness has value for all things, holding promise for both the present life and the life to come" (1 Timothy 4:7-8, NIV).

For exercise to be effective, it needs to be consistent and focused. Simply hanging out at the gym while chatting and checking out others accomplishes nothing. Paul's words are again instructive. "Do you not know that in a race all the runners run, but only one gets the prize? Run in such a way as to get the prize. Everyone who competes in the games goes into strict training. They do it to get a crown that will not last, but we do it to get a crown that will last forever. Therefore I do not run like someone running aimlessly; I do not fight like a boxer beating the air. No, I strike a blow to my body and make it my slave so that after I have preached to others, I myself will not be disqualified for the prize" (1 Corinthians 9:24-27, NIV).

Paul trained to win. He was diligent and relentless. I encourage you to embrace these disciplines of prayer, fasting and giving with similar determination. Do not simply suffer through them. Grab on to them and expect great results. Before you know it you will experience renewed freedom, life and empowerment.

Before we move on I have a word of caution. Refuse to turn life-giving principles into legalistic demands. Regenerate is not focused on what I cannot do, rather on what I can do. It is not about what I can accomplish through self-determination and self-discipline, but what I can receive from His grace. We are letting go of a few things for a few days to embrace something better. We are letting go to lay hold; practicing hard to win games; denying self to become our true self. Refuse to give up. Do not beat yourself up if you stumble. If you fall down, get back up and try again. If you cannot do everything, do something. Always remember, something is better than nothing.

> *Something is better than nothing.*

Regenerate is the launching pad for you to walk unfettered in the freedom Christ has for you. Embrace the disciplines!

Discussion Questions

1. When you hear the word discipline what comes to mind? Is it a positive, negative or neutral word?

2. How have you experienced spiritual discipline to be liberating, life-giving and empowering?

3. How can life-giving principles turn into legalistic demands? How do we guard against this?

CHAPTER SIX

_____

From Triple Threat To Victory

From Triple Threat To Victory

To escape the hurt and pain from growing up with an abusive father I started drinking at age 15, eventually becoming an alcoholic for over 20 years. Thanks to Jesus I have over 9-1/2 years of sobriety. I have learned to experience security and joy when I keep my eyes on Him and not my circumstances.
- Carlos

Great victory typically requires great effort. If success were easy, everyone would be successful. Whether it is business, marriage, career, athletics or ministry success comes with a price. *"This*

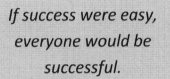

If success were easy, everyone would be successful.

kind can come out by nothing but prayer and fasting" (Mark 9:29, NKJV). *"This kind"* of bondage does not break easily; *"this kind"* of problem is not simply solved; *"this kind"* of obstacle is not effortlessly moved. A sudden burst of enthusiastic courage, even in the name of the Lord, does not always cause the enemy to flee in fear. David's words to Goliath were bold and full of faith, "You come against me with sword and spear and javelin, but I come against you in the name of the LORD Almighty, the God of the armies of Israel, whom you have defied. This day the LORD will deliver you into my hands, and I'll strike you down and cut off your head. This very day I will give the carcasses of the Philistine army to the birds and the wild animals, and the whole world will know that there is a God in Israel. All those gathered here will know that it is not by sword or spear that the LORD saves; for the battle is the LORD's, and he will give all of you into our hands" (1 Samuel 17:45-47, NIV).

Wow! Those are strong words of faith (They would have scared me off!). So did David's initial burst of faith intimidate his problem and cause it to go away? Nope, Goliath was a *"this kind"* of giant. The next verse says, "As the Philistine moved closer to attack him…" (1 Samuel 17:48, NIV). Not only did the giant problem not run away, it ran toward him. The already huge giant must have seemed to actually grow in size as it drew nearer.

The old adage, "things will get worse before they get better," may not always be true, but sometimes it can sure seem that way. Regenerate is not an easy fix to life's giant problems. A sudden burst of faith in God and courageous rebuke of the enemy seldom results in our problems simply melting away. Most of the time we still have to face our enemy in battle. This is not the result of a lack of faith. It is simply the reality of spiritual warfare. David, you will remember, persevered in his faith. David ran toward the approaching Goliath and 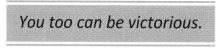 killed him. You too can be victorious.

They say things come in threes — A B C's; small, medium, large; Tic-Tac-Toe; yada, yada, yada; blah, blah, blah; thank you, thank you, thank you. Any time a celebrity or two dies, the rest get nervous. Like most superstitions, I doubt this principle of three is invariably true, but it certainly describes the plight of King Jehoshaphat. The king and the people of Judah were facing not one, not two, but three powerful enemies — the proverbial triple threat. "After this, the Moabites and Ammonites with some of the Meunites came to make war on Jehoshaphat" (2 Chronicles 20:1, NIV). The only thing missing were the Gesundheits!

The situation was mega-serious — it was a *"this kind"* of problem. Not just one foe, but three, ganging up with a view to destroy. There are times we think things cannot possibly get worse only to discover our troubles are just beginning. After fighting every inch of the way to make it through a bad economy we get laid off. A recession is when you lose your job; a depression is when I lose mine! Next comes a bad report from the doctor. To top it off, we discover our spouse has left us. Jehoshaphat knows how we feel, and we can learn from his response. "Alarmed, Jehoshaphat resolved to inquire of the LORD, and he proclaimed a fast for all Judah" (2 Chronicles 20:3, NIV).

Notice Jehoshaphat's instinctive reaction. It was an all too human reaction of fear, alarm and even terror. I say, "Good for Jehoshaphat." It shows he is not a paper hero on a paper page, but a real person just like you and me. This was literally a life and death situation. Without divine intervention the men would soon be dead, the women raped and the children carried into captivity. Thankfully his *reaction* was different than his *response*. He did not allow his instinctive reaction of fear to control his actions. Though tempted to panic and rush into action he hit the pause button so he could stop and first seek God. For

Jehoshaphat, seeking God was not a matter of last resort, but first choice.

> *Seeking God was not a matter of last resort, but first choice.*

Regenerate is an invitation to hit the pause button and seek the Lord. Whether it is a taunting giant adversary moving toward us or a triple threat surrounding us it is difficult not to cave into our instincts and immediately react. However, many of the things we stress over would fall into proper perspective if we would pursue His plan before rushing into action. "But seek first the kingdom of God and his righteousness, and all these things shall be added to you" (Matthew 6:33, NKJV).

The next step the king took was to declare a fast. In this instance a fast pointed to the intensity needed to face such a dire emergency. This required a beyond the normal call of duty time of prayer and seeking God. If they ever needed divine intervention, it was now.

Along with seeking God and fasting, Jehoshaphat led the people in prayer. He did not delegate the responsibility to the professional priests, but led the prayer himself. Some things cannot be delegated to others! The triple threat was met by a triple response: 1) seeking God; 2) fasting; and 3) prayer. Jehoshaphat's prayer is a model of intercession.

"Then Jehoshaphat stood up in the assembly of Judah and Jerusalem at the temple of the LORD in the front of the new courtyard and said: 'LORD, the God of our ancestors, are you not the God who is in heaven? You rule over all the kingdoms of the nations. Power and might are in your hand, and no one can withstand you. Our God, did you not drive out the inhabitants of this land before your people Israel and give it forever to the descendants of Abraham your friend? They have lived in it and have built in it a sanctuary for your Name, saying, "If calamity comes upon us, whether the sword of judgment, or plague or famine, we will stand in your presence before this temple that bears your Name and will cry out to you in our distress, and you will hear us and save us."

"'But now here are men from Ammon, Moab and Mount Seir, whose territory you would not allow Israel to invade when they came from Egypt; so they turned away from them and did not destroy them. See how they are repaying us by coming to drive us out of the possession You gave us as an inheritance. Our God, will you not judge them? For we have no power to face this vast army that is attacking us. We do not know what to do, but our eyes are on you'" (2 Chronicles 20:5-12, NIV).

Like the triple threat and the triple response, Jehoshaphat's prayer is another triple. He asks God three questions: 1) Are you not? (verse 6); 2) Did you not? (verse 7); and 3) Will you not? (verse 12). Jehoshaphat begins by reminding God of His mighty power. He is the Creator and Ruler of the universe. He then tells the Lord how over the centuries He has delivered Judah's ancestors from calamities, plagues, famines and enemies. News alert — prayer is not giving God unknown information. He already knows who He is and what He has done. God does not have a self-image problem. He does not need to be pumped up or sweet-talked into doing something for us. Rather, this type of declarative prayer reminds the one praying of God's ability and power. God's track record of faithfully caring for His people builds hope for the present and the future. Not only the king, but the entire nation of Judah had their own faith stirred up by the prayer declarations.

Having reminded God of who He is and what He has done, Jehoshaphat gets to the point with his third question, "Will You not?" In other words, "God, do it again!" The king then confesses their complete lack of power. In fact he states quite candidly that they do not have the slightest idea what to do. If God does not intervene, they are toast. The only thing they know to do is look to Him.

As you begin Regenerate, you too may encounter overwhelming troubles you are powerless to face. You may be clueless as to what to do. But by seeking God first with prayer and fasting you will discover His plan of rescue.

> *By seeking God first with prayer and fasting you will discover His plan of rescue.*

rescue. Jehoshaphat and the people of Judah did. Their awareness sharpened in the quiet of pursuing Him empowered them to hear a word through a prophet. "Do not be afraid or discouraged because of this vast army. For the battle is not yours, but God's... Take up your positions; stand firm and see the deliverance the LORD will give you... Do not be afraid; do not be discouraged. Go out to face them tomorrow, and the LORD will be with you" (2 Chronicles 20:15, 17, NIV). If they did their part, God would do what they could not — His part. God did not declare the triple threat would simply vanish, but He did promise His presence and His power. If they would stand firm in the midst of their impossible situation, God would fight for them. They were not to be afraid of "*this kind*" of problem.

Having heard from God, the king took the lead and forcefully proclaimed, "Have faith in the LORD your God and you will be upheld; have faith in his prophets and you will be successful" (2 Chronicles 20:20, NIV). God's promise of deliverance still required faith to receive on the part of the people. With the king firmly committed to God's promise, the people too responded in faith.

At this point it is instructive to note that Jehoshaphat and the people did not simply close their eyes and passively wait for a miracle. God had told them to take their place and stand firm. But what did that mean for them? "After consulting the people, Jehoshaphat appointed..." (2 Chronicles 20:21, NIV). The king did not issue an edict (faith cannot be commanded); rather he consulted with the people as to the best way to proceed. In short, together they developed a strategy. A promised miracle typically requires activity on our part. A financial breakthrough still requires money strategies. A relationship miracle still necessitates doing the things that build rather than destroy. A healing miracle may still mean doctors' visits and medical treatments.

Of course at times strategies birthed out of prayer and fasting may seem a bit odd. It certainly did in this case. "After consulting the people, Jehoshaphat appointed men to sing to the LORD and to praise him for the splendor of his holiness as they went out at the head of the army, saying: 'Give thanks to the LORD, for his love endures forever'" (2 Chronicles 20:21, NIV). What was that again? The choir, armed with nothing more than praise, was to march in front of the army. Who would place a choir in front of the military when marching out to battle? It is probably good that Jehoshaphat consulted with the people before asking them to go with a plan like this. This would not have made sense to someone without faith, and probably a few with faith wondered if this were really what God meant. If this were not a God thing they would be history.

The strategy employed actually has a solid spiritual truth underpinning it. Praise always precedes the victory. Praise is faith in action. Praise invites the presence of God. Say what you want — it worked! "As they began to sing and praise, the LORD set ambushes against the men of Ammon and Moab and Mount Seir... And the kingdom of Jehoshaphat was at peace, for his God had given him rest on every side" (2 Chronicles 20:22, 30, NIV).

God gave him victory and with victory came rest! So if you feel ganged up on, if you feel surrounded on every side, do not despair. Your first reaction may be fear. But make your first response seeking God in prayer. Allow your faith in Him to result in praise as you move forward to face your enemy. God is able to turn a deadly triple threat into a great victory. If God is for you, who can be against you?

If God is for you, who can be against you?

Discussion Questions

1. "A sudden burst of faith in God and courageous rebuke of the enemy seldom results in our problems simply melting away. Most of the time we still have to face our enemy in battle. This is not the result of a lack of faith. It is simply the reality of spiritual warfare." Have you found this to be true in your life?

2. In what way can you relate to the story of Jehoshaphat? How does it encourage you?

3. "Praise always precedes the victory." What does this look like in your specific situation(s)?

CHAPTER SEVEN

The Sophomore Challenge

The Sophomore Challenge

I left an abusive relationship but never healed from it. I thought that God was finished with me; that He had no use for me. In coming to Faith I learned about God's forgiveness, grace and mercy and discovered a family that cheers me on.
- Brooke

The only good thing about being a sophomore is you are no longer a punky freshman. Even then, as the name itself implies, at least being a freshman has the advantage of everything seeming "fresh" and new. While often a little scary, freshman year has the excitement of a new campus, new courses, new students, new teachers, and new possibilities. Besides, it is always easier to start than to finish, whether it is a diet or pursuing a degree. By year two, however, the initial rush of enthusiasm is long gone only to be replaced by the recognition of how much work it actually takes to finish just one year of school. Then comes a most disturbing realization — you are not yet even halfway done and the hard road ahead is longer than the road behind. By junior year there is the advantage of being an upperclassman. Lots of hard work still to do but now you are more than half way through with the end in sight. Senior year? Not without its challenges, but basically a piece of cake compared to the other three. Short of disaster, graduation is imminent. For me, it is that second year, the sophomore year, which holds the biggest motivational challenges.

Do not be surprised if you encounter the sophomore challenge during Regenerate. Although we are talking forty days, not four years, the same process applies. The first few days, while dreadfully difficult for some, may seem like "no problemo" for others. The natural excitement and freshness of trying new things might carry you along with the hopeful thought, "Maybe this time it'll work." Soon, however, since long-term difficulties and stubborn destructive habits may be confronted, the realization kicks in that this is not going to be a walk in the park. Initially hoping for a quick and easy miracle it becomes apparent that "*this kind*" of problem is going to require some major effort. The temptation to throw in the towel and go back to old comfortable routines grows. The giant is not going away, but moving toward you!

The sophomore challenge capitalizes on weariness. We are tired from the effort it has already taken to make it this far. We are tired just thinking about how much farther we have to go. When we are tired and worn out it is easy to lose focus and lose hope. The great football coach Vince Lombardi said, "Fatigue makes cowards of us all." We are tempted to think, "This thing may work for others, but I just can't do this!" If we do not give up hope altogether, we might get anxious and start looking for short cuts or compromises. Aware of this human tendency Paul writes, "And let us not grow weary while doing good, for in due season we shall reap if we do not lose heart" (Galatians 6:9, NKJV).

Paul knew firsthand the challenge of pressing on in faith despite seemingly insurmountable odds. Here is just a sampling of what Paul faced after deciding to pursue his destiny in God.

Paul knew firsthand the challenge of pressing on in faith despite seemingly insurmountable odds.

"Five times I received from the Jews the forty lashes minus one. Three times I was beaten with rods, once I was pelted with stones, three times I was shipwrecked, I spent a night and a day in the open sea, I have been constantly on the move. I have been in danger from rivers, in danger from bandits, in danger from my fellow Jews, in danger from Gentiles; in danger in the city, in danger in the country, in danger at sea; and in danger from false believers. I have labored and toiled and have often gone without sleep; I have known hunger and thirst and have often gone without food; I have been cold and naked. Besides everything else, I face daily the pressure of my concern for all the churches" (2 Corinthians 11:24-28, NIV).

What a list! Any one of these things would have caused most to throw up their hands in despair and quit. But Paul was no quitter. From a jail cell in Rome he declared,

"... I press on to take hold of that for which Christ Jesus took hold of me. Brothers and sisters, I do not consider myself yet to have taken hold of it. But one thing I do: Forgetting what is behind and straining toward what is ahead, I press on toward the goal to win the prize for which

God has called me heavenward in Christ Jesus" (Philippians 3:12-14, NIV).

To gain victory over the sophomore challenge we too must "press on." Much of Paul's past caused him shame, guilt and regret. Once he even called himself the "worst" sinner (1 Timothy 1:15). His past, especially after he came to Christ, was also filled with victories and unique revelations that could have caused him to rest on his laurels. But Paul refused to focus on the past, whether it included his victories or failures. Neither shame nor pride would stop him from fighting through the dark times and pressing on to victory. Paul was focused on where he was going — his destiny.

No one can successfully move forward focused on the rearview mirror. When backing up the car or changing lanes mirrors are essential, but even then they are no substitute for turning our heads for a direct line of sight. The rearview mirror is a helpful tool that needs to be glanced at while otherwise our eyes are fixed on where we are going. Have you ever tried to drive your car forward while looking in the rearview mirror? Just keeping the vehicle going straight is tricky, not to mention it is an accident waiting to happen. Even if it were possible to safely drive with eyes gazing in the rearview mirror, progress would be exceptionally slow and getting off course would be the norm. We can learn from our past, we can gain perspective from our past, but

We need to get "past our past" and press on.

the time comes when we need to get "past our past" and press on.

When the going gets tough it is tempting to romanticize the past. We miss the "good ole days" before we were committed to giving up, starting up and stepping up. We could eat what we wanted when we wanted and how we wanted. Were not Sundays for sleeping in and watching football rather than hassling getting the kids ready for church? At the same time we forget the pain of abusive relationships or destructive addictions, or maybe just the emptiness of life without God. The Israelites fell prey to such thinking while wandering through the wilderness. God had rescued them from four hundred years of oppressive bondage in Egypt and through Moses was leading them to the Promised Land. They had much to be thankful for and to look forward to. But in between, when they grew tired and hungry and were not sure how much longer they would be in the wilderness, they started to idealize Egypt. At least in Egypt they had a roof over their heads, food to eat and water to drink. Now they faced daily challenges and an uncertain future. Many wanted to go back to Egypt, preferring having basic needs met while slaves to the challenges that come with freedom, liberty and opportunity. In the end, the sophomore challenge caused an entire generation of God's people to give up and fall short of their destiny. It was left for a new generation to enter the Promised Land.

Paul refused to romanticize his past. Before coming to Christ, Paul had been a big shot — "a Hebrew of Hebrews" he remembered — but now he considered all the awards and accolades as "rubbish" compared to pursuing Christ. Paul was not about to allow anything to distract him, be it shame and guilt or comfort and pride. Like me, Paul loved sports and learned to take the posture of an athlete, straining forward, eyes focused on the finish line. When the initial endorphin rush of the start of the race wore thin and weariness settled in, he learned to press on through the sophomore challenge and keep going. At the end of his life he was able to say, "I have fought the good fight, I have finished the race, I have kept the faith" (2 Timothy 4:7, NKJV).

Jesus said, "Ask, and it will be given to you; seek, and you will find; knock, and it will be opened to you" (Matthew 7:7, NKJV). In the original language the verbs connote continuous action. In other words, ask and keep on asking, seek and keep on seeking, knock and keep on knocking. During my youth ministry days our church had a door to door witnessing program. It was cold turkey stuff, no referrals or previously interested parties here. I am quite shy by nature and had it not been for the fact I was on staff I do not think I could have handled going to strange houses, knocking on strange doors and talking to strange people. As it was, I distinctly remember often knocking lightly once or twice on the door hoping the inhabitants were not home so I could move on. Such fearful caution is the exact opposite of the determination Jesus was noting. God rewards the diligent, the persistent. Keep asking. Keep seeking. Keep knocking.

Pressing on is especially difficult when hard work seems to produce no results. Often, however, more is happening than what appears. For example, when planting a seed in a garden it may be days, even weeks, before the seed sprouts. Very little, if any, visible results of the hard work of prepping the soil, planting, watering and fertilizing are immediately apparent. As a child I remember planting carrot seeds in our garden and expecting to see an edible vegetable the next morning. Disappointment grew day after day as I saw nothing but dirt. Finally, when something did appear it looked more like a green weed than an orange carrot. I was convinced whatever I had done had not worked. My parents assured me otherwise. Sure enough, the day came when my mom pulled the "green weed" out of the ground and there it was — my orange carrot.

What is happening when nothing seems to be? Just like with seed, God is often working in our lives "below the surface." Whether it is people or circumstances, or both, He is developing a root system capable of handling the inevitable breakthrough. God's timing is perfect. Exercise patience and trust Him. The Bible exhorts us in this regard, "... do not become sluggish, but imitate those who through faith and

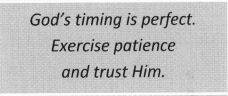

God's timing is perfect. Exercise patience and trust Him.

patience inherit the promises" (Hebrews 6:12-13, NKJV).

Decide in your heart right now that come hell or high water you are not going to quit pursuing God. Do not delay the decision until the tough times come — decide before they arrive. Contrary to common assumption, the Bible never says "God helps those who help themselves," but it does have a promise for those who never give up. Paul exhorts us to "work out your own salvation with fear and trembling," but he quickly adds, "...for it is God who works in you both to will and to do for his good pleasure"

(Philippians 2:12-13, NKJV). Note two things: 1) we can only work out what God has first worked in; and 2) whether it is waning will-power or lack of ability God will supply what is needed as long as we do not quit. God is committed to helping us as we press through the sophomore challenge to victory.

Discussion Questions

1. Have you ever encountered the sophomore challenge while pursuing God? What was that like? How did you overcome it?

2. Paul wrote about forgetting what lies in the past. Is there anything from your past (victories or failures) that you have not yet left behind? What would it look like for you to "forget" the past and press on toward the goal and through the sophomore challenge?

CHAPTER EIGHT

Point Of Grace

Point Of Grace

I was orphaned at birth in Africa and set apart to die by the tribal elders as they believed I was the cause of my mother's death. My uncle rescued me and I was adopted and raised by a Christian missionary woman. After her death I realized I wasn't living up to God's purpose for my life. In coming to Faith I have discovered that God saved me as an infant to do great things for Him.
- John

While great breakthrough typically requires time and effort on our end, we should never doubt the power of God to bring about radical change in an instant. If we do not lose heart and

> *Never doubt the power of God to bring about radical change in an instant.*

continue to press through we will eventually reach a point of grace that brings miraculous victory — a gateway out of living in the natural into the supernatural. Before we wondered if it was ever going to happen. Now things move so fast we wonder, "What happened?" We wake up in the morning and everything is business as usual, but by the time we go to bed a major shift, like a spiritual earthquake, has occurred. We have experienced our point of grace where everything has changed.

As a teenager Joseph had a dream that one day he would be a ruler with his brothers bowing down to him. Everyone already knew he was his daddy's favorite so such a grandiose dream did not sit well with his brothers. After almost killing him, they sold him into slavery and Joseph ended up in Egypt. Serving faithfully he was falsely accused of rape and sexual harassment. For years he languished in prison for a crime he did not commit. His gift of interpreting dreams helped others get out of jail but once free they forgot about him. Joseph helped others with their dreams, but what about his? Serving time in prison is especially hard if one has no idea when, or even if, he will ever get out. But Joseph never gave up hope. Finally, seemingly out of the blue, Joseph experienced a point of grace.

Waking up one ordinary morning in jail Joseph was suddenly brought before Pharaoh who was troubled by nightmares. Joseph was not only able to interpret the dreams he also knew the proper course of action for the nation. This so impressed Pharaoh that he put Joseph in charge of Egypt, his powers second only to Pharaoh himself. Think about that — Joseph woke up in the morning a prisoner, and by the time he went to bed that same night he was in charge of the nation! What seemed like something that would never happen occurred all in one day. To bring things full cycle, Joseph's brothers traveled from Canaan to Egypt because of a famine and ended up bowing before him as an Egyptian ruler. They did not recognize him at first but Joseph soon revealed himself and the family healing began. Joseph's God-given dream ended up being not about personal ambition or self-promotion but about the salvation of a family and a nation.

From prison to the palace in one day — we find this pattern of sudden, surprising breakthrough over and over again in the scriptures. Hannah had long sought the Lord regarding having a child, only to see others blessed year after year while she remained barren. But she never gave up. One day her prayers were so emotionally intense Eli accused her of being drunk. This particular prayer, however, was the one that moved heaven to act on her behalf. She conceived and gave birth to a son who would grow up to judge and lead the nation — Samuel. Hannah experienced a point of grace.

Unlike Hannah who never gave up the Bible tells about a wealthy Shunammite woman who had given up all hope of ever having a child. Surprisingly she was not bitter and actually had a pretty good life, thank you very much. She was a big supporter of Elisha's ministry and helped provide for his needs whenever he was in town. To thank her for her faithful service Elisha asked what he could do to bless her. She humbly responded that all her needs were met. Later informed she was childless, Elisha prophesized over her that in a year she would be holding her own baby in her arms. Having already dealt with the personal pain of bareness and not wanting to resurrect false hopes, the woman was hesitant. Still, in one year she was indeed nursing her own son. She experienced a point of grace.

Yet another woman who had been bleeding for twelve years sneaked up behind Jesus, who was being pressed on all sides by the crowd, and with much effort was finally able to touch the hem of His garment. Her frustration level must have been at an all time high as she had spent all her money on doctors who could not help her. In fact, the bleeding was worse than ever. Now she was not only sick, she was both sick and broke! But she did not give up hope. The moment she touched the Lord's cloak the bleeding immediately stopped. Jesus, having felt power flow out of Him, asked His disciples, "Who touched Me?" They were amazed by the question and Peter responded, "Look at the crowds, like EVERYBODY is touching You!" (Reeve translation). But Jesus meant a different kind of touch — a touch of faith. He said to the woman in tender terms, "Daughter, be of good cheer; your faith has made you well. Go in peace" (Luke 8:48, NKJV). She experienced a point of grace.

Reaching a point of grace is not reserved for females only. Life had not been kind to Blind Bartimaeus. As were many handicapped people of that time he was consigned to fending for himself as a beggar, totally dependent on the generosity of others just to make it through the day. When he heard that Jesus was passing through he cried out for mercy. The crowd tried to shush him but he refused to be silenced and shouted all the more. His persistence paid off. Jesus did indeed stop, took notice of his needs, and healed him. What began as another normal day of a blind man begging ended up with Bartimaeus going to bed at night with restored vision. He experienced a point of grace.

Peter was sound asleep chained between two guards after being thrown in prison by King Herod. James, brother of John, had just been beheaded due to the intense persecution so things were not looking too good for Peter. I am amazed he could sleep at all given the circumstances. Maybe it was the result of his friends praying, for the Bible tells us, "While Peter was being kept in jail, the church never stopped praying to God for him" (Acts 12:5, CEV). God answered their prayers with yet another "suddenly" — He sent an angel to personally escort Peter out of jail. When Peter showed up at the front door of the prayer meeting, the people were so shocked they thought it was a ghost and not really him! Peter and the church experienced a point of grace.

Like Peter, Paul found himself in a dark, dirty prison cell with his co-worker Silas. They had already been "severely flogged" so they had every reason to be in a foul mood. Unlike Peter, they were not sleeping even when midnight rolled around, but neither were they worried, complaining or mired in self-pity. Instead, with the other prisoners listening they were praying and singing praises to God (not too sure that is what I would have been doing). The Bible teaches that praise precedes the victory and praise invites the presence of God. It certainly did in this case. God sent an earthquake,

> *Praise precedes the victory and praise invites the presence of God.*

locked doors sprung open and shackles came off. Paul and Silas, sensitive to the guidance of the Holy Spirit, did not simply rush out — the Lord had more in mind than their deliverance. When the jailor awakened and realized what had happened, he was going to kill himself since he would be executed anyway for allowing prisoners to escape. But Paul shouted, "Don't harm yourself! We are all here" (Acts 16:28, NIV). A relieved jailor asked what he needed to do to be saved and Paul responded with now famous words, "Believe in the Lord Jesus, and you will be saved — you and your household" (Acts 16:31, NIV). Paul, Silas, the jailor and his family experienced a point of grace.

Abraham was already seventy-five years old when he first received the incredible promise that he would be the father of nations. If that were not enough, almost twenty-five years later with Abraham approaching one hundred years of age and Sarah well past childbearing years, there was still no child on the horizon. No fertility clinics, no Viagra, Cialis or Levitra, only a promise from God. Paul describes Abraham's faith and commitment during these challenging years, "Without weakening in his faith, he faced the fact that his body was as good as dead — since he was about a hundred years old — and that Sarah's womb was also dead. Yet he did not waver through unbelief regarding the promise of God, but was strengthened in his faith and gave glory to God, being fully persuaded that God had power to do what he had promised" (Romans 4:19-21, NIV). Though it took years Abraham and Sarah finally encountered their point of grace.

The stories and details may differ, but our spiritual forefathers and foremothers have much in common. They did not allow their circumstances to quell their worship, harden their heart, quench their passion, silence their faith or hinder their service. They pressed through until they reached their point of grace. The same God who did it for them is still working His grace today and is able to do it for you!

> *God is still working His grace today and is able to do it for you!*

Discussion Questions

1. Have you ever experienced a "point of grace" in your life? What did it look like? How did it occur?

2. Which of the point of grace examples referenced in this chapter encourage you the most?

CHAPTER NINE

Traveling Companion

Traveling Companion

I had it all - marriage, family, education and career, but I wasn't happy. Through a series of bad choices my life fell apart and I found myself humiliated as a welfare recipient. My mother encouraged me to receive help from a local church and I soon began attending Faith where my life turned around. I found the happiness I was looking for and a circle of friends to do life with.
- Anna

Facing our giants can be quite intimidating. When the time comes to move from big talk to big action it is good to know we are not alone. This forty-day journey can be taken with your spouse, your family, your friends, your coworkers, or your small group. One mentor I

> *When the time comes to move from big talk to big action it is good to know we are not alone.*

would encourage all to take along as a traveling companion is David. If anyone knows about slaying giants it is David! But there is more to it than that. David is the only person about whom the Bible specifically states was a man after God's own heart. Wow! What a reputation. On the other hand, though it is easy to view David and other biblical characters like mythic heroes, the reality is they were ordinary human beings just like you and me. David experienced rejection, betrayal, dysfunction, loss, and failure. What if we could sit down with him over a cup of coffee and talk about life? Since his story and poetry are preserved in the scriptures we have the opportunity to learn from him even though our lives are separated by thousands of years. We will be spending time daily in the book of Psalms, many of which were written by David.

When you think of the Psalms what image first comes to mind? For me, I imagine a young shepherd boy playing a harp while watching his sheep graze in a beautiful meadow with green grass. The scene is serene, pleasant and uplifting. Perhaps this is due to the most famous of all the Psalms — "The Lord is my shepherd; I shall not want. He makes me to lie down in green pastures; He leads me besides the still waters. He restores my soul" (Psalm 23:1-3, NKJV). However, the Psalms reflect the full gamut of human drama, emotion and adventure. Many of the Psalms deal with issues like betrayal, abandonment, guilt, shame, doubt and fear. While on the cross in deep agony Jesus quoted David's cry of alienation, "My God, my God, why have you forsaken me" (Psalm 22:1, NIV)? In the Psalms we sense David's passion, we feel his pain, we rejoice in his victories and we struggle with his questions.

Since many of the Psalms are connected with specific instances in David's life, some background on him may provide context and greater insight for your readings in the Psalms.

David's Faith Was Forged In The Wilderness

Stepping out of our comfort zone for forty days may feel like we are leaving the comforts of home to embark on a wilderness experience. For me, staying in the wilderness would seem more of a punishment than an adventure. Do not get me wrong; I am willing to "rough it" all day as long as I have a comfortable bed to sleep in at night, preferably at a five-star hotel. Marguerite, on the other hand, loves to backpack and can sleep on the ground under the stars with nothing more than a sleeping bag. Whether you embrace the adventure of the wilderness or dread its discomforts, there is no disputing its challenges and opportunities.

David spent much of his formative years in the wilderness. The youngest of Jesse's sons, like a brand new employee, David was given the jobs and the hours nobody else wanted. Lonely days and nights watching sheep could have resulted in monotonous boredom. Instead, David invested his time composing and singing songs of adoration and praise to God. He stayed alert despite the all-night shifts and was therefore ready when encountering dangerous situations that tested his skills. The abilities as a warrior that would later cause him to become a national hero were honed as a young shepherd fighting off bears, lions and any other wild animals looking for fast food. He was a faithful protector of the little flock that had been placed under his care. David may not have thought much about it at the time, but he was in training to lead men.

As demanding as it may seem at times, the wilderness can be a better place for our development than life as usual in the comfort of our home. It is unlikely David would have grown into the champion he became staying

> *The wilderness can be a better place for our development than life as usual.*

in a home environment where he was stereotyped as the runt. His brothers questioned his abilities and motivation. His father never even considered that he might be the one Samuel was looking for to anoint the next king of Israel. At best David was overlooked; at worst he was forgotten. But God had neither overlooked nor forgotten David. God was not only sharpening David's skills as a warrior and leader in the wilderness, He was developing David's character. The faith that was forged in the wilderness served as his foundation for the remainder of his life.

> *The faith that was forged in the wilderness served as his foundation for the remainder of his life.*

David's Hope Was Rooted In God's Faithfulness

David's introduction to the world at large came after slaying Goliath. He became an instant celebrity and his new found fame spread like wildfire. It seemed as if David's time had come and Samuel's prediction of his destiny as king soon would be fulfilled. David's road to destiny, however, would involve some interesting and unexpected twists. One person not too thrilled with David's overnight fame was King Saul. The top tunes sung by the beautiful maidens were no longer centered around the handsome king, but around the exploits of the new kid on the block. Saul's insecurities turned to jealousy and finally into uncontrollable rage. Despite David's faithful service to his nation and his king, Saul became consumed with killing him. Saul tried to pin David to the wall with a spear while David was serenading the king with a harp. Only David's quickness enabled him to dodge the spear. This happened not once, but twice! Eventually things grew so bad David had to leave town and go on the run. Once again, he found himself in the wilderness. How discouraging this must have been — ending up right where he started.

Some of David's Psalms were written while on the run from Saul. We hear his cry for justice. Despite God's promise that he would be the next king of Israel, he had to wait patiently for the promise to be fulfilled while loyally serving King Saul and the people of Israel. He had done nothing wrong! They say no good deed goes unpunished, but why should he have to run and hide in holes and caves like an animal? When would he be vindicated? When would the promise be fulfilled? Where was his breakthrough? Perhaps you can relate.

While on the run David soon was joined by a band of men the Bible describes as "in distress or in debt or discontented" (1 Samuel 22:2, NIV). This was quite the motley crew, comprised of misfits, losers and probably a few outlaws. David became the leader of these approximately four hundred men and it was not long until they began to change. Eventually these same men were transformed into David's mighty men, performing their own miraculous exploits and even killing giants as big and bad as Goliath. These men experienced regeneration — total spiritual transformation. You can too.

One day it appeared God had answered David's cries for deliverance. While David and his men were hiding deep in a cave with King Saul and the army in pursuit, Saul innocently went into the same cave to relieve himself. Talk about being in a vulnerable position — Saul was an easy target. David's men saw this as an obvious answer to prayer and fully expected their leader to kill the man trying to kill him. But David refused. He sensed while this may be a good opportunity, it was not a God opportunity. His faith in God's promise and desire to be king did not mean he should force the issue or attempt in his own strength to make things happen. Saul was the current king, the Lord's anointed. It was God's job to deal with Saul. David would not only wait on the Lord by seeking His will through prayer, he would also wait for the Lord by patiently submitting to God's timing and plan.

What enabled David to "keep on keepin' on" when it seemed everything was stacked against him? How could he wait and not jump at opportunities others saw as chances not to be missed? He had learned that genuine hope in God does not, in the end, disappoint.

> *Genuine hope in God does not, in the end, disappoint.*

"I waited patiently for the LORD; and He inclined to me, and heard my cry. He also brought me up out of a horrible pit, out of the miry clay, and set my feet upon a rock, and established my steps. He has put a new song in my mouth — praise to our God; many will see and fear, and trust in the LORD" (Psalm 40:1-3, NKJV). At the right time and in the right way, David became king.

David Unashamedly Worshipped God

At the core Regenerate is about pursuing the presence of God. No one knew more about seeking God than David. One of the first things David did as king was recapture Jerusalem so he could bring the Ark of the Covenant back to Zion. David and Israel knew God was bigger than a box, but the ark did represent God's presence in a powerful and unique way. Not surprisingly during the reign of King Saul the Ark had been neglected. Refreshment, renewal, revival — yes, regeneration — was needed for the nation to reach its full potential. The new king and the nation wanted and needed God's presence.

David had learned as a young shepherd that praise invites the presence of God. Now that he was a sophisticated king he was not about to let go of the power of praise. David the warrior had taught the people how to prevail in battle; now David the worshipper would model for them how to prevail with God through prayer, sacrifice, and radical praise. "And so it was, when those bearing the ark of the LORD had gone six paces, that he sacrificed oxen and fatted sheep. Then David danced before the LORD with all his might; and David was wearing a linen ephod. So David and all the house of Israel brought up the ark of the LORD with shouting and with the sound of the trumpet" (2 Samuel 6:13-15, NKJV).

Every six paces they stopped, sacrificed and worshipped! Not the fastest, cheapest, or most convenient way to get the job done, but David knew the importance of taking time to pursue God. If you are too busy for God, you are too busy! It was not really an expenditure of time, effort and finances, but an investment in the nation's future. Note too that David was not concerned with what anyone thought. He gladly took off his "fit for the red carpet" kingly garments and danced in common clothes so that attention was not focused on him, but God. He was not trying to win *Dancing With The Stars*; he was pointing the people to the ultimate Superstar.

Those closest to us are occasionally not thrilled with our decision to change our lives and pursue the Lord. David's own wife Michal blasted her husband the king for getting so exuberant in his celebrations. Michal came from royalty, having been raised in a king's house, and knew about class and political correctness. She warned him about his "fanaticism." David was undeterred. "It was before the LORD," he retorted, "I will celebrate before the LORD." It was not about his honor, rather about HIS honor. Then he tells his wife she has not seen anything yet, "I will become even more undignified than this, and I will be humiliated in my own eyes" (2 Samuel 6:21-22, NIV). It is tough when people you love and care about do not understand your passion for God. But David would not be deterred. He was a warrior and he was a worshipper!

David Demonstrated Authentic Repentance

David was a man of passion, and a few times his passion led to trouble — big trouble. The classic example is the time he was on his rooftop enjoying a warm spring evening when he saw a UFO — an Unclad Female Object. The beautiful woman David saw bathing was Bathsheba, the wife of one of his best soldiers, a man named Uriah. The king should have been out to war with his men but for whatever reason he had remained at home. David was undeterred by the news the bathing beauty was married. He had her brought to him anyway and, to make a long story short, he became a babydaddy (I think that is what the tabloids call it).

Like with Watergate and Lewinskygate, attempts at cover-up grew worse than the original sin. In David's case lies led to betrayal, which in turn led to murder. Still, David did not repent until confronted by the prophet Nathan. Finally, the man after God's own heart stopped the masquerade and radically repented. Psalm fifty-one is the result of this episode and presents a classic model of repentance, prayer, forgiveness and restoration. Countless millions over the centuries have echoed David's heart. "Create in me a clean heart, O God, and renew a steadfast spirit within me. Do not cast me away from Your presence, and do not take Your Holy Spirit from me. Restore to me the joy of Your salvation, and uphold me by Your generous Spirit" (Psalm 51:10-12, NKJV). When push came to shove, David did not run away from God in his guilt and shame — he ran to God.

> *David did not run away from God in his guilt and shame — he ran to God.*

Let David mentor you as you give up, start up, and step up to pursue God away from the limitations of life as usual. The challenges of your wilderness will liberate you from limitations as you discover the person God intended you to be. Let David encourage you to slow down and wait in hope for God to unfold His plan as He leads you through the valley to victory. Let David challenge you to raise your level of prayer and worship as you focus not on your own dignity but His glory. Finally, let David comfort those devastated by personal failure and sin with the assurance that forgiveness, renewal and restoration is available if we will only run to God rather than away from Him.

Discussion Questions

1. If you were to go out to coffee with King David what question would you most like to ask him?

2. How have you experienced God using wilderness experiences to build your faith?

3. "Praise invites the presence of God." What circumstances in your life are currently in need of God's presence? What might it look like for you to praise Him in the midst of these situations?

REGENERATE

A PILGRIMAGE OF THE HEART

40-DAY DEVOTIONAL

WRITTEN BY: PASTOR DAWN JACKSON
FAITH COMMUNITY CHURCH

Regenerate — A Pilgrimage Of The Heart

Are you hungry to go deeper in your relationship with God? Are you ready to cut away the things which are unnecessary, to be free from that which distracts and hinders so that you experience God's presence in a fresh and new way? This devotional is a forty-day journey through Psalms. It is a place of prayer, contemplation, reflection and seeking after the very face of God. With honesty and by God's grace we become, like the Psalmist himself, a people after God's own heart.

The devotional is divided into four parts:

Part One: Longings
Part Two: Preparation
Part Three: Declaration
Part Four: The Climb

Each day you will be presented with a scripture, a reflection and a prayer. Before you start, ask God to open your heart to hear what He has to say to you that day. Prayerfully read the scripture and allow the reflection to challenge your thoughts. Utilize the prayer as a launching point for the cry of your own heart. Jesus spent His forty-day experience in the wilderness. While it is unrealistic for us to go and spend forty days in a literal wilderness, we can bring the wilderness to you. How you combine these elements is up to you. This is your journey. It is your pilgrimage of the heart.

Part One: Longings

Longing is defined as a strong feeling of wanting something. It is to yearn, to desire, to crave. During these first six days, allow for God to stir the longings of your heart for regeneration.

Day 1   Longings
Regenerate

Psalm 95, NLT

Come, let us sing to the LORD! Let us shout joyfully to the Rock of our salvation. Let us come to him with thanksgiving. Let us sing psalms of praise to him. For the LORD is a great God, a great King above all gods. He holds in his hands the depths of the earth and the mightiest mountains. The sea belongs to him, for he made it. His hands formed the dry land, too. Come, let us worship and bow down. Let us kneel before the LORD our maker, for he is our God. We are the people he watches over, the flock under his care. If only you would listen to his voice today! The LORD says, "Don't harden your hearts as Israel did at Meribah, as they did at Massah in the wilderness. For there your ancestors tested and tried my patience, even though they saw everything I did. For forty years I was angry with them, and I said, 'They are a people whose hearts turn away from me. They refuse to do what I tell them.' So in my anger I took an oath: 'They will never enter my place of rest.'"

Reflection

Today, we set out upon a pilgrimage of the heart — a forty-day journey of regeneration. To regenerate means to be formed again; to undergo spiritual rebirth or renewal. The Psalmist cautions us against hard, unbelieving hearts. Rather we are invited into an amazing relationship with God; one characterized by praise, thanksgiving, worship and the recognition of His Lordship in the world and in our lives. What needs to be regenerated in your life today? What condition is your heart in? Take time today to prayerfully examine your heart. How will you respond to the invitation to come, sing, shout and worship?

Prayer

Examine my heart, Lord. Reveal to me areas, which are hard that I might surrender them to You. And as I surrender I know that You will take that which is stone and regenerate it so that it becomes alive and vibrant. Today I hear Your invitation to come, and so I come. I come to praise You. I come to worship You. I come to surrender to You.

Day 2   **Longings**
Yearning

Psalm 27, NLT

The LORD is my light and my salvation — so why should I be afraid? The LORD is my fortress, protecting me from danger, so why should I tremble? When evil people come to devour me, when my enemies and foes attack me, they will stumble and fall. Though a mighty army surrounds me, my heart will not be afraid. Even if I am attacked, I will remain confident. The one thing I ask of the LORD — the thing I seek most — is to live in the house of the LORD all the days of my life, delighting in the LORD's perfections and meditating in his Temple. For he will conceal me there when troubles come; he will hide me in his sanctuary. He will place me out of reach on a high rock. Then I will hold my head high above my enemies who surround me. At his sanctuary I will offer sacrifices with shouts of joy, singing and praising the LORD with music. Hear me as I pray, O LORD. Be merciful and answer me! My heart has heard you say, "Come and talk with me." And my heart responds, "LORD, I am coming." Do not turn your back on me. Do not reject your servant in anger. You have always been my helper. Don't leave me now; don't abandon me, O God of my salvation! Even if my father and mother abandon me, the LORD will hold me close. Teach me how to live, O LORD. Lead me along the right path, for my enemies are waiting for me. Do not let me fall into their hands. For they accuse me of things I've never done; with every breath they threaten me with violence. Yet I am confident I will see the LORD's goodness while I am here in the land of the living.

Wait patiently for the LORD. Be brave and courageous. Yes, wait patiently for the LORD.

Reflection

What is the thing which you seek most? The things of this world are temporary yet we often think that by attaining them we will have peace. Some things which we pursue are not healthy for us. Others are more neutral, neither good nor bad in and of themselves. Then there are those things which are good. However, there is only one thing which will fulfill our deepest longing; the thing the Psalmist sought most — a vibrant, personal relationship with God. The NIV translates verse 8 in this way:

"My heart says of you, 'Seek his face!' Your face, Lord, I will seek."

Jesus taught us that if we seek first His Kingdom everything else would be taken care of. Remember playing the game hide and seek as a child. How much effort would you put into seeking your friends when they were hiding from you? Well the good news is God is not hiding from you. He wants to be found. And if we will seek Him with all our hearts He will reveal himself in ways we may have never experienced before. The Lord's goodness awaits you. Wait patiently for the Lord.

Prayer

Lord God, today the cry of my heart is to seek Your face. I desire to know You in a deeper way than I have ever known You before. My heart yearns for You. You are the foundation of my life — my light and my salvation. You are the source of my joy, my purpose and my life. Only You satisfy my deepest longing. I know that as I keep You first You will take care of the other needs of my life. Today, I wait patiently for You.

Day 3   **Longings**
Grace

Psalm 145, MSG

I lift you high in praise, my God, O my King! and I'll bless your name into eternity. I'll bless you every day, and keep it up from now to eternity. God is magnificent; he can never be praised enough. There are no boundaries to his greatness. Generation after generation stands in awe of your work; each one tells stories of your mighty acts. Your beauty and splendor have everyone talking; I compose songs on your wonders. Your marvelous doings are headline news; I could write a book full of the details of your greatness. The fame of your goodness spreads across the country; your righteousness is on everyone's lips. God is all mercy and grace — not quick to anger, is rich in love. God is good to one and all; everything he does is suffused with grace. Creation and creatures applaud you, God; your holy people bless you. They talk about the glories of your rule, they exclaim over your splendor, Letting the world know of your power for good, the lavish splendor of your kingdom. Your kingdom is a kingdom eternal; you never get voted out of office. God always does what he says, and is gracious in everything he does. God gives a hand to those down on their luck, gives a fresh start to those ready to quit. All eyes are on you, expectant; you give them their meals on time. Generous to a fault, you lavish your favor on all creatures. Everything God does is right — the trademark on all his works is love. God's there, listening for all who pray, for all who pray and mean it. He does what's best for those who fear him — hears them call out, and saves them. God sticks by all who love him, but it's all over for those who don't. My mouth is filled with God's praise. Let everything living bless him, bless his holy name from now to eternity!

Reflection

God is all mercy and grace. Wow! Mercy is not getting what we do deserve; namely the punishment for the things which we have done wrong. Grace is getting the good things that we do not deserve. It is God's unmerited favor. We have been saved by His grace. We didn't (couldn't) earn it. It was a gift. It is also by His grace that we are transformed. In our own power we cannot change. Yet by His grace we can experience victory in our life in a new and fresh way. The Psalmist recounts how he has witnessed God's grace. How have you personally experienced the working of God's grace? Are you ready for God to unleash His gracious acts in your life? Don't try to work for it. Don't try to be good enough to merit it. Don't disqualify yourself thinking you don't measure up. Simply receive it and walk in it.

Prayer

Father, I long for Your grace in my life. Too often I strive and toil trying to run my life with my own strength. There have been times when I have tried to earn Your favor; earn Your love. But Your love is unconditional. I have done nothing to deserve it. Freely You have given it to me. Unleash Your grace in my life. Bring life to the areas of my heart which have been calloused by my anxious and self-serving ways. By faith I receive Your work of grace in my life.

Day 4   **Longings**
Truth

Psalm 19, NLT

The heavens proclaim the glory of God. The skies display his craftsmanship. Day after day they continue to speak; night after night they make him known. They speak without a sound or word; their voice is never heard. Yet their message has gone throughout the earth, and their words to all the world. God has made a home in the heavens for the sun. It bursts forth like a radiant bridegroom after his wedding. It rejoices like a great athlete eager to run the race. The sun rises at one end of the heavens and follows its course to the other end. Nothing can hide from its heat. The instructions of the LORD are perfect, reviving the soul. The decrees of the LORD are trustworthy, making wise the simple. The commandments of the LORD are right, bringing joy to the heart. The commands of the LORD are clear, giving insight for living. Reverence for the LORD is pure, lasting forever. The laws of the LORD are true; each one is fair. They are more desirable than gold, even the finest gold. They are sweeter than honey, even honey dripping from the comb. They are a warning to your servant, a great reward for those who obey them. How can I know all the sins lurking in my heart? Cleanse me from these hidden faults. Keep your servant from deliberate sins! Don't let them control me. Then I will be free of guilt and innocent of great sin. May the words of my mouth and the meditation of my heart be pleasing to you, O LORD, my rock and my redeemer.

Reflection

God's Word is true. His laws, demands and decrees are the reality by which we need to live to fully experience life. Truth is often like a gardening tool which digs around in our life exposing that which needs to be uncovered so it can be removed. Truth can be uncomfortable and often we try to avoid it, rationalizing our behavior. But, it is truth that sets us free. And your heart — your heart longs to be free. Perhaps the truth of God needs to invade your relationships, your finances, your work habits, your hobbies. As you nurture this longing in your heart to go deeper with God, allow His Spirit of truth to probe your heart for any areas in need of some attention. Don't allow rationalization or excuses to rob you of the future God has for you.

Prayer

Lord, Your commands are good. They bring life to my soul. Spirit of truth I invite you to invade my heart. Shine Your light into the dark recesses of my soul. Give me direction that I might live according to Your Word and walk in the freedom that You offer me.

Day 5   Longings
Winter

Psalm 42:1-4, NLT

As the deer longs for streams of water, so I long for you, O God. I thirst for God, the living God. When can I go and stand before him? Day and night I have only tears for food, while my enemies continually taunt me, saying, "Where is this God of yours?" My heart is breaking as I remember how it used to be: I walked among the crowds of worshippers, leading a great procession to the house of God, singing for joy and giving thanks amid the sound of a great celebration!

Reflection

The Psalmist remembered how it used to be. Our life is comprised of seasons. Some seasons are fruitful. Other seasons feel like the dead of winter when we remember what it was like to not be where we currently find ourselves. In our seasons of winter we practice what is known as naked faith. The "feel goods" are gone. We press on simply because we know it is the right thing to do. There does not appear to be much life, in fact there can be a bone chilling dryness. But, it is in times like these that our faith grows. A tree in winter appears to be dead, yet underneath the surface flows life and the simple hint of spring causes it to burst into leaf. If you are in a winter season, be encouraged. Spring for your soul is right around the corner.

Prayer

Lord, I long for spring. Warm the areas of my heart which are cold. Bring Your life giving rains to moisten that which is dry and dusty. Yet, I am reminded that just because I can't see or feel Your power at work in me does not mean You are not there. So, while I am in this season do a deep work in my life. And, I will follow You whether I feel like it or not because You are God and I know that You are good.

Day 6   **Longings**
Hope

Psalm 42:5-11, NLT

Why am I discouraged? Why is my heart so sad? I will put my hope in God! I will praise him again — my Savior and my God! Now I am deeply discouraged, but I will remember you — even from distant Mount Hermon, the source of the Jordan, from the land of Mount Mizar. I hear the tumult of the raging seas as your waves and surging tides sweep over me. But each day the LORD pours his unfailing love upon me, and through each night I sing his songs, praying to God who gives me life. "O God my rock," I cry, "Why have you forgotten me? Why must I wander around in grief, oppressed by my enemies?" Their taunts break my bones. They scoff, "Where is this God of yours?" Why am I discouraged? Why is my heart so sad? I will put my hope in God! I will praise him again — my Savior and my God!

Reflection

Today's reading was the second half of the chapter we began yesterday where the Psalmist was remembering how things used to be and longing to return to the presence of God. As he found himself downcast and discouraged he made a great choice. He put his hope in God. In the New Testament, we find that hope acts like an anchor for our soul. There will be times in life when we will face storms. These may be storms we have brought on ourselves by making bad decisions. Sometimes we encounter storms caused by the poor choices of other people. Then there are storms which happen simply because we live in a fallen world. But with our soul anchored to Jesus, our rock, we will be held fast. Today, if you are facing any type of discouragement, anchor yourself to Christ. He is your living hope.

Prayer

Lord Jesus, today I place all my hope in You. I am confident that You will hold me fast through the storms of life. I can hope in You because You are faithful, able and willing to fulfill every promise You have made. Therefore, I will trust You with all my heart.

Part Two: Preparation

Our heart is set on pilgrimage; a desire to go to new levels in our relationship with God. Yet, like any journey, preparations must be made before we leave. During these next two weeks allow for God to do a deep work in your heart through prayer, fasting and sacrifice.

Day 7   Preparation
Beginnings

Psalm 37:1-7, NIV

Do not fret because of those who are evil or be envious of those who do wrong; for like the grass they will soon wither, like green plants they will soon die away. Trust in the LORD and do good; dwell in the land and enjoy safe pasture. Take delight in the LORD, and he will give you the desires of your heart. Commit your way to the LORD; trust in him and he will do this: He will make your righteous reward shine like the dawn, your vindication like the noonday sun. Be still before the LORD and wait patiently for him; do not fret when people succeed in their ways, when they carry out their wicked schemes.

Reflection

Trust in the Lord... Delight yourself in the Lord... Commit your way to the Lord... Be still before the Lord... What a great way to begin this process of preparing yourself for regeneration. Take some time today to meditate on each of these phrases. What does it look like for you to trust, delight, commit and be still? As you approach God have an open and willing heart to do whatever He instructs you to do today.

Prayer

Lord, I ask that You would prepare me for what lies ahead. I want to be renewed. Correct me in areas where I am trusting in people or things rather than in You. You are the source of true joy and Your way is higher than my way. So I quiet myself before You, that I might hear Your Spirit speak to me. I am open for You to do Your work in my life.

Day 8   Preparation
Prayer

Psalm 61, NLT

O God, listen to my cry! Hear my prayer! From the ends of the earth, I cry to you for help when my heart is overwhelmed. Lead me to the towering rock of safety, for you are my safe refuge, a fortress where my enemies cannot reach me. Let me live forever in your sanctuary, safe beneath the shelter of your wings! For you have heard my vows, O God. You have given me an inheritance reserved for those who fear your name. Add many years to the life of the king! May his years span the generations! May he reign under God's protection forever. May your unfailing love and faithfulness watch over him. Then I will sing praises to your name forever as I fulfill my vows each day.

Reflection

How often have you heard the statement, "Well I guess all I can do about it is pray"? For those who desire a vibrant spiritual life, prayer should not be the last resort. Prayer is our lifeline to God. It is open communication to call upon the Creator of the universe and invite Him to take action in our lives. As David struggled with his circumstances he looked to God to be his refuge and he cried out to Him in prayer. Prayer was his first response. There are many different elements to prayer — praise, confession, thanksgiving, supplication, intercession. Some of these we will look at over the next few days. However, to keep things from getting too complicated remember that prayer is simply talking to God. When you talk to Him be real just like the writers of the Psalms who felt no need to sugarcoat their situations or feelings. Be relaxed as prayer is not a formality. Allow your heart to open up to the heart of God and dialogue with Him.

Prayer

Lord, today I want to be real with You. Here is where I struggle. Here is what I do not understand. I open my heart to You. I look to You fully assured that You hear my prayer. I put my hope in You for You are faithful, You are able and You are good.

Day 9   Preparation
Praise

Psalm 148, NLT

Praise the LORD! Praise the LORD from the heavens! Praise him from the skies! Praise him, all his angels! Praise him, all the armies of heaven! Praise him, sun and moon! Praise him, all you twinkling stars! Praise him, skies above! Praise him, vapors high above the clouds! Let every created thing give praise to the LORD, for he issued his command, and they came into being. He set them in place forever and ever. His decree will never be revoked. Praise the LORD from the earth, you creatures of the ocean depths, fire and hail, snow and clouds, wind and weather that obey him, mountains and all hills, fruit trees and all cedars, wild animals and all livestock, small scurrying animals and birds, kings of the earth and all people, rulers and judges of the earth, young men and young women, old men and children. Let them all praise the name of the LORD. For his name is very great; his glory towers over the earth and heaven! He has made his people strong, honoring his faithful ones — the people of Israel who are close to him. Praise the LORD!

Reflection

Praise invites God's presence to invade our circumstances. It is made up of adoration and thanksgiving. Adoration is simply adoring (or admiring) God for who He is; that He is good, He is powerful, He is able. In praising Him, we magnify Him. When you use a magnifying glass you make an object appear larger than it really is. But when we magnify God, we do not make Him bigger, rather we begin to see how big He actually is. This both builds our faith and honors God who is worthy of our praise. Today, spend time adoring God for who He has revealed Himself to be in your life.

Prayer

Father, You have revealed Yourself to me in so many ways. You are my savior, my provider, my healer, my shepherd. You are all powerful; nothing is impossible for You. You are also good and can be trusted. You are filled with mercy and grace. With my entire soul I praise You. You alone are worthy of all praise!

Day 10   Preparation
Confession

Psalm 32, NLT

Oh, what joy for those whose disobedience is forgiven, whose sin is put out of sight! Yes, what joy for those whose record the LORD has cleared of guilt, whose lives are lived in complete honesty! When I refused to confess my sin, my body wasted away, and I groaned all day long. Day and night your hand of discipline was heavy on me. My strength evaporated like water in the summer heat. Finally, I confessed all my sins to you and stopped trying to hide my guilt. I said to myself, "I will confess my rebellion to the LORD." And you forgave me! All my guilt is gone. Therefore, let all the godly pray to you while there is still time, that they may not drown in the floodwaters of judgment. For you are my hiding place; you protect me from trouble. You surround me with songs of victory. The LORD says, "I will guide you along the best pathway for your life. I will advise you and watch over you. Do not be like a senseless horse or mule that needs a bit and bridle to keep it under control." Many sorrows come to the wicked, but unfailing love surrounds those who trust the LORD. So rejoice in the LORD and be glad, all you who obey him! Shout for joy, all you whose hearts are pure!

Reflection

Sin which is not confessed is a roadblock to our pilgrimage. In the Psalm, David said he was miserable, his strength sapped as in summer heat, when he refused to confess his sin. But once he confessed his sin, he found relief. Confession literally means to say the same thing as.

In other words, to say the same thing as God says about our behavior when it is out of alignment with His Word. We are not to sugar coat it and act like it is not a big deal. We are to take it seriously. In fact, cherishing sin in our hearts can be a hindrance to our prayers. Today, invite the Holy Spirit to search your heart and reveal any area of disobedience that has not been dealt with. Once revealed, simply confess the sin as sin and ask God for His forgiveness. And He is faithful; He will forgive you.

Prayer

Holy Spirit, search my heart. Expose my excuses, rationalization and rebellion and reveal to me any areas where I have been disobedient to Your Word. And I know that as I confess these things, You will forgive me. Thank You for setting me free.

Day 11   Preparation
Repentance

Psalm 51, NLT

Have mercy on me, O God, because of your unfailing love. Because of your great compassion, blot out the stain of my sins. Wash me clean from my guilt. Purify me from my sin. For I recognize my rebellion; it haunts me day and night. Against you, and you alone, have I sinned; I have done what is evil in your sight. You will be proved right in what you say, and your judgment against me is just. For I was born a sinner — yes, from the moment my mother conceived me. But you desire honesty from the womb, teaching me wisdom even there. Purify me from my sins, and I will be clean; wash me, and I will be whiter than snow. Oh, give me back my joy again; you have broken me — now let me rejoice. Don't keep looking at my sins. Remove the stain of my guilt. Create in me a clean heart, O God. Renew a loyal spirit within me. Do not banish me from your presence, and don't take your Holy Spirit from me. Restore to me the joy of your salvation, and make me willing to obey you. Then I will teach your ways to rebels, and they will return to you. Forgive me for shedding blood, O God who saves; then I will joyfully sing of your forgiveness. Unseal my lips, O Lord, that my mouth may praise you. You do not desire a sacrifice, or I would offer one. You do not want a burnt offering. The sacrifice you desire is a broken spirit. You will not reject a broken and repentant heart, O God. Look with favor on Zion and help her; rebuild the walls of Jerusalem. Then you will be pleased with sacrifices offered in the right spirit — with burnt offerings and whole burnt offerings. Then bulls will again be sacrificed on your altar.

Reflection

We have confessed our sin but we must also repent. To repent is to make a 180 degree turn and go the other way. It is a conscious choice to change our behavior for today and in the future. Some of our struggles may have become strongholds and we are in need of others to help us in overcoming these destructive patterns. To repent in these areas would mean to pursue the support you need, such as recovery groups, counseling or accountability with another strong believer. What does repentance look like for you today? What choices do you need to make as you turn to go the other way? You might also consider sharing with someone else the choices you are making so as to have the support you need to follow through.

Prayer

Lord, today I repent and choose to turn around and walk according to Your Word. I know that Your Holy Spirit empowers me with Your grace. And it is Your grace which enables me to change. In the areas where I struggle, help me to get connected to other believers who will support me in my transformation. I desire for every aspect of my life to reflect You.

Day 12   Preparation
Forgiveness

Psalm 103, NLT

Let all that I am praise the LORD; with my whole heart, I will praise his holy name. Let all that I am praise the LORD; may I never forget the good things he does for me. He forgives all my sins and heals all my diseases. He redeems me from death and crowns me with love and tender mercies. He fills my life with good things. My youth is renewed like the eagle's! The LORD gives righteousness and justice to all who are treated unfairly. He revealed his character to Moses and his deeds to the people of Israel. The LORD is compassionate and merciful, slow to get angry and filled with unfailing love. He will not constantly accuse us, nor remain angry forever. He does not punish us for all our sins; he does not deal harshly with us, as we deserve. For his unfailing love toward those who fear him is as great as the height of the heavens above the earth. He has removed our sins as far from us as the east is from the west. The LORD is like a father to his children, tender and compassionate to those who fear him. For he knows how weak we are; he remembers we are only dust. Our days on earth are like grass; like wildflowers, we bloom and die. The wind blows, and we are gone — as though we had never been here. But the love of the LORD remains forever with those who fear him. His salvation extends to the children's children of those who are faithful to his covenant, of those who obey his commandments! The LORD has made the heavens his throne; from there he rules over everything. Praise the LORD, you angels, you mighty ones who carry out his plans, listening for each of his commands.

Yes, praise the LORD, you armies of angels who serve him and do his will! Praise the LORD, everything he has created, everything in all his kingdom. Let all that I am praise the LORD.

Reflection

You have been forgiven! God does not count your sins against you anymore. David writes that our sins have been removed as far away from us as the east is from the west. If you look at a globe, you can see that east and west never meet (unlike north and south). The Bible says that there is no condemnation for those that are in Christ Jesus. So don't allow for yourself to be trapped by shame or guilt, thinking that God must have a second rate plan for your life. No! Jesus took your shame on Him and paid the price for your sin. You have been justified and made righteous. Walk in that forgiveness and allow yourself to fully experience His love, mercy and grace.

Prayer

Father, thank You for Your forgiveness. Thank You for removing all my shame and guilt and making me righteous. I bask in Your love and mercy. I thrive in Your grace. You are so good to me. I love You, Lord.

Day 13   Preparation
Thanksgiving

Psalm 100, NLT

Shout with joy to the LORD, all the earth! Worship the LORD with gladness. Come before him, singing with joy. Acknowledge that the LORD is God! He made us, and we are his. We are his people, the sheep of his pasture. Enter his gates with thanksgiving; go into his courts with praise. Give thanks to him and praise his name. For the LORD is good. His unfailing love continues forever, and his faithfulness continues to each generation.

Reflection

As mentioned before, praise is made up of both adoration and thanksgiving. So often we take for granted the blessings which God brings into our life. But, we have so much to be grateful for! Today, spend time thinking through all the ways God has blessed your life and enter the gates of God's presence with a prayer of thanksgiving from your heart.

Prayer

Lord, I acknowledge that all good things come from You. I don't want to take anything for granted. Today, I reflect upon all the blessings You have poured into my life. You have been so very good to me and I am eternally grateful.

Day 14
Fasting

Psalm 132:1-5, TNIV

LORD, remember David and all his self-denial. He swore an oath to the LORD and made a vow to the Mighty One of Jacob: "I will not enter my house or go to my bed, I will allow no sleep to my eyes or slumber to my eyelids, till I find a place for the LORD, a dwelling for the Mighty One of Jacob."

Reflection

We find various kinds of fasts in the Bible. In today's Psalm, David spoke of denying himself sleep as he pursued a dwelling place for the presence of God. Other types of fasts include food or some type of activity. The purpose of this time is not to draw attention to ourselves or to attempt to manipulate God. Rather, this period of denial allows for us to focus in on a deeper walk with God. It humbles us as we learn to rely on God for strength, provision and wisdom. What type of a fast has God called you to during this forty-day season? What is your fast teaching you about God? This season of fasting is an incredible opportunity to really press in to your relationship with God.

Prayer

Father, as I deny myself during this season of fasting, I do it for the sole purpose of seeking Your face and acknowledging that You are the source of my life. Lord, I want to go deep in my relationship with You. You are the one who sustains me.

Day 15   **Preparation**
Contemplation

Psalm 139, NLT

O LORD, you have examined my heart and know everything about me. You know when I sit down or stand up. You know my thoughts even when I'm far away. You see me when I travel and when I rest at home. You know everything I do. You know what I am going to say even before I say it, LORD. You go before me and follow me. You place your hand of blessing on my head. Such knowledge is too wonderful for me, too great for me to understand! I can never escape from your Spirit! I can never get away from your presence! If I go up to heaven, you are there; if I go down to the grave, you are there. If I ride the wings of the morning, if I dwell by the farthest oceans, even there your hand will guide me, and your strength will support me. I could ask the darkness to hide me and the light around me to become night — but even in darkness I cannot hide from you. To you the night shines as bright as day. Darkness and light are the same to you. You made all the delicate, inner parts of my body and knit me together in my mother's womb. Thank you for making me so wonderfully complex! Your workmanship is marvelous — how well I know it. You watched me as I was being formed in utter seclusion, as I was woven together in the dark of the womb. You saw me before I was born. Every day of my life was recorded in your book. Every moment was laid out before a single day had passed. How precious are your thoughts about me, O God. They cannot be numbered! I can't even count them; they outnumber the grains of sand! And when I wake up, you are still with me! O God, if only you would destroy the wicked!   Get out of my life, you murderers!   They blaspheme you; your enemies misuse your name.   O LORD, shouldn't I hate those who hate you?   Shouldn't I despise those who oppose you?   Yes, I hate them with total hatred, for your enemies are my enemies.   Search me, O God, and know my heart; test me and know my anxious thoughts. Point out anything in me that offends you, and lead me along the path of everlasting life.

Reflection

Spending time in prayer and fasting provides us with the opportunity to contemplate God's character and power. To contemplate is to think deeply on a subject. In this Psalm, David contemplates God's omniscience (the fact that He knows everything) and His omnipresence (the fact that God is present everywhere). Other Psalms contemplate God's omnipotence (the fact that He is all powerful). Use today's Psalm as a model for your own reflection of God's character and power.

Prayer

As I meditate upon You, Lord I am filled with wonder. You are so amazing, so powerful and so wise. Nothing escapes You. Your thoughts are higher than my thoughts. Your ways are higher than my ways. You are altogether magnificent and I am humbled by Your presence.

Day 16
Hunger

Preparation

Psalm 63, NLT

O God, you are my God; I earnestly search for you. My soul thirsts for you; my whole body longs for you in this parched and weary land where there is no water. I have seen you in your sanctuary and gazed upon your power and glory. Your unfailing love is better than life itself; how I praise you! I will praise you as long as I live, lifting up my hands to you in prayer. You satisfy me more than the richest feast. I will praise you with songs of joy. I lie awake thinking of you, meditating on you through the night. Because you are my helper, I sing for joy in the shadow of your wings. I cling to you; your strong right hand holds me securely. But those plotting to destroy me will come to ruin. They will go down into the depths of the earth. They will die by the sword and become the food of jackals. But the king will rejoice in God. All who trust in him will praise him, while liars will be silenced.

Reflection

As we fast and contemplate God, we realize just how hungry we are for more of Him. Nothing can satisfy this hunger except God Himself. In the New Testament, Jesus said that man does not live on bread alone but on every word which proceeds from the mouth of God. And God is good, for He fills and satisfies us. At times you will find your body craving the food or activity you have given up during this season. Use that craving to re-focus your attention on God. Allow your hunger to drive you to Him.

Prayer

Lord, like the Psalmist I thirst and hunger for You! Only You can fill me. I have tried other things but they have left me wanting more. You are the one who gives meaning to my life. You have created me and given my life purpose. You are my protector and the source of my security. I hunger for more of You in my life.

Day 17   Preparation
Focus

Psalm 119:9-24, NLT

How can a young person stay pure? By obeying your word. I have tried hard to find you — don't let me wander from your commands. I have hidden your word in my heart, that I might not sin against you. I praise you, O LORD; teach me your decrees. I have recited aloud all the regulations you have given us. I have rejoiced in your laws as much as in riches. I will study your commandments and reflect on your ways. I will delight in your decrees and not forget your word. Be good to your servant, that I may live and obey your word. Open my eyes to see the wonderful truths in your instructions. I am only a foreigner in the land. Don't hide your commands from me! I am always overwhelmed with a desire for your regulations. You rebuke the arrogant; those who wander from your commands are cursed. Don't let them scorn and insult me, for I have obeyed your laws. Even princes sit and speak against me, but I will meditate on your decrees. Your laws please me; they give me wise advice.

Reflection

Fasting has a way of focusing our attention on God. That which is peripheral fades away. The mind is clear. All that remains is what is most important. Focus is powerful. A laser, which can cut through steel or perform a delicate surgery, is actually focused light. A focused walk with God is also powerful and fasting helps to enable that. Without focus we may find ourselves distracted and making little headway or impact in life. During seasons of fasting, God's voice is heard more clearly, His direction more easily discerned. His Word comes alive and fills our life with truth. The author of today's Psalm found himself completely dependent on God's Word. It was the heartbeat of his life empowering him to live purely and purposefully before God. How is God using this season to focus your life?

Prayer

How good it is to focus in on You. As I worship, I have come to find that nothing compares to You. The cares and concerns of this world fade away. No longer distracted I give my full attention to You. Lord, show me Your way. Teach me Your Word. I want to know You more and live my life completely for You.

Day 18   **Preparation**
Sacrifice

Psalm 4:5, NIV

Offer the sacrifices of the righteous and trust in the LORD.

Psalm 50:14-15, NIV

"Sacrifice thank offerings to God, fulfill your vows to the Most High, and call on me in the day of trouble; I will deliver you, and you will honor me."

Psalm 50:23, NIV

"Those who sacrifice thank offerings honor me, and to the blameless I will show my salvation."

Psalm 76:11, NIV

Make vows to the LORD your God and fulfill them; let all the neighboring lands bring gifts to the One to be feared.

Reflection

Today's scriptures are excerpts from a few different Psalms. In the days of the Old Testament, the Israelites would sacrifice different types of animals to God for various purposes. Some were for the purpose of worship and some were used to atone for their sin. Regardless of the purpose of the sacrifice, that which was brought was to be without blemish; the animal could not have a defect. They would also offer the best of the first fruits of their harvest to God. God deserved their best. In bringing God their first fruits, it acknowledged that the entire harvest was from the Lord and belonged to Him. During this season of regeneration, we are also bringing sacrifices to God. These sacrifices may consist of the giving of our time, our talent and/or our financial resources. But, it is a sacrifice and not simply a contribution. Of course the motivation for our sacrifice is not guilt or manipulation but rather love. Our expectation is that God will bless us. How are you doing in sacrificing to God? How has this season of giving personally challenged and encouraged you?

Prayer

Father, I acknowledge that all that I have, my strength, time, talent, resources, etc. belong to You. During this season I bring to You my sacrifice and I am grateful for the opportunity. Use what I bring to You to honor Your name and to build Your Kingdom. Thank You for accepting my sacrifice.

Day 19   Preparation
Devoted

Psalm 119:105-112, NLT

Your word is a lamp to guide my feet and a light for my path. I've promised it once, and I'll promise it again: I will obey your righteous regulations. I have suffered much, O LORD; restore my life again as you promised. LORD, accept my offering of praise, and teach me your regulations. My life constantly hangs in the balance, but I will not stop obeying your instructions. The wicked have set their traps for me, but I will not turn from your commandments. Your laws are my treasure; they are my heart's delight. I am determined to keep your decrees to the very end.

Reflection

We often call the time we spend praying and reading the Bible our "devotions," which is appropriate as devotions can be defined as a religious observance. But, devotion is deeper than simply an observance. To be devoted is to have a profound dedication to something which one strongly admires or is enthusiastic about. It is to be earnestly attached to a cause or a person. In today's Psalm, we read, "I've promised it once and I'll promise it again..." The Message translates this as "I've committed myself and I'll never turn back." We live in a day and age when commitments are often not taken seriously. Personal commitments, business commitments, marriage commitments — many are quite easily broken. To be devoted is to be so dedicated that nothing can or ever will break this commitment. We find the writers of the Psalms to be men who had deep devotion to God. In today's reading, the Psalmist's devotion to God's Word was unparalleled. God's Word provided the direction for his life and brought him delight. Even under threat from his enemies he would not stop obeying God's law or turn from God's commandments. How would you describe your devotion to God and His Word?

Prayer

Father, regardless of what others say or think, regardless of the shallowness of the times in which I live when people give their word and then break it, I am devoted to You and nothing will ever change that. I commit myself completely and fully to You. I am determined to walk according to Your Word.

Day 20   Preparation
Cost

Psalm 109:1-5, NIV

My God, whom I praise, do not remain silent, for people who are wicked and deceitful have opened their mouths against me; they have spoken against me with lying tongues. With words of hatred they surround me; they attack me without cause. In return for my friendship they accuse me, but I am a man of prayer. They repay me evil for good, and hatred for my friendship.

Psalm 109:21-31, NIV

But you, Sovereign LORD, help me for your name's sake; out of the goodness of your love, deliver me. For I am poor and needy, and my heart is wounded within me. I fade away like an evening shadow; I am shaken off like a locust. My knees give way from fasting; my body is thin and gaunt. I am an object of scorn to my accusers; when they see me, they shake their heads. Help me, LORD my God; save me according to your unfailing love. Let them know that it is your hand, that you, LORD, have done it. While they curse, may you bless; may those who attack me be put to shame, but may your servant rejoice. May my accusers be clothed with disgrace and wrapped in shame as in a cloak. With my mouth I will greatly extol the LORD; in the great throng of worshippers I will praise him. For he stands at the right hand of the needy, to save their lives from those who would condemn them.

Reflection

As you have pursued this regeneration of your heart through fasting, prayer and sacrifice, you may have encountered some people who are not as excited about your decision to press on in your faith. There is often a cost associated in pursuing God. The Psalmist faced people speaking ill of him and attacking him without cause. Even those he had treated as friends falsely accused him. In your journey, you might find yourself ridiculed and isolated. While we believe for God's favor in our lives, there are times when we pay a price for being people of faith. But know that if and when this occurs, you are in good company. The Psalmist experienced it. The disciples experienced it. Jesus experienced it. And, in God's timing you will be vindicated.

Prayer

Lord, whatever the cost I will follow You. When I am under attack or treated poorly because of my faith I will remember that at times You Yourself were treated this way. I will trust You to vindicate me rather than trying to accomplish that with my own hands. While I know that I walk with Your favor on my life, when life requires that I pay a price for my faith I will pay it.

Part Three: Declaration

Your heart is prepared for the journey but there is one more thing to do before departing. When Daniel found himself as a young man in Babylon, he resolved not to defile himself. He made a decision ahead of time as to how he would behave and he lived his entire life in alignment with that decision. These next few days will provide you with the opportunity to make your own declarations about who you are in Christ and how you will live.

Day 21   **Declaration**
Pruning

Psalm 86, NIV

Hear me, LORD, and answer me, for I am poor and needy. Guard my life, for I am faithful to you; save your servant who trusts in you. You are my God; have mercy on me, Lord, for I call to you all day long. Bring joy to your servant, Lord, for I put my trust in you. You, Lord, are forgiving and good, abounding in love to all who call to you. Hear my prayer, LORD; listen to my cry for mercy. When I am in distress, I call to you, because you answer me. Among the gods there is none like you, Lord; no deeds can compare with yours. All the nations you have made will come and worship before you, Lord; they will bring glory to your name. For you are great and do marvelous deeds; you alone are God. Teach me your way, LORD, that I may rely on your faithfulness; give me an undivided heart, that I may fear your name. I will praise you, Lord my God, with all my heart; I will glorify your name forever. For great is your love toward me; you have delivered me from the depths, from the realm of the dead. Arrogant foes are attacking me, O

God; ruthless people are trying to kill me — they have no regard for you. But you, Lord, are a compassionate and gracious God, slow to anger, abounding in love and faithfulness. Turn to me and have mercy on me; show your strength in behalf of your servant; save me, because I serve you just as my mother did. Give me a sign of your goodness, that my enemies may see it and be put to shame, for you, LORD, have helped me and comforted me.

Reflection

If you have ever grown roses, you know that they need to be pruned back (not simply clipped) on an annual basis. When a plant or tree is pruned, it does not look very good but it is vital for its continued health. Proper pruning accomplishes a few things. First, it maintains the health of the plant by removing what is dead or diseased. Second, it directs the growth of the plant so as to maximize its potential. Next, it increases the quality and yield of the fruit. And finally, it positions the plant so as to ensure it has a strong structure. David's experience of being hunted by Saul as David lived in the wilderness was used by God as a time to prune him and prepare him for God's call on his life to be the next king of Israel. Through the pruning process he was completely dependent on God as he found himself to be poor and in need. During this process of preparation, you have been pruned by prayer, fasting and sacrifice. That which is unnecessary has been cut off. Your growth has been directed and you have been positioned for strength. You are now ready for a fruitful season. You might feel a little vulnerable and exposed but soon you will break into bloom.

Prayer

Lord, You have pruned me. You have cut me back and I am in a vulnerable place completely dependent on You. I know that this pruning was not done in vain. You have a purpose for my life and I humbly wait upon You. Because of this process, I will be stronger and ready for a fruitful season.

Day 22   **Declaration**
Decision

Psalm 26, NLT

Declare me innocent, O LORD, for I have acted with integrity; I have trusted in the LORD without wavering. Put me on trial, LORD, and cross-examine me. Test my motives and my heart. For I am always aware of your unfailing love, and I have lived according to your truth. I do not spend time with liars or go along with hypocrites. I hate the gatherings of those who do evil, and I refuse to join in with the wicked. I wash my hands to declare my innocence. I come to your altar, O LORD, singing a song of thanksgiving and telling of all your wonders. I love your sanctuary, LORD, the place where your glorious presence dwells. Don't let me suffer the fate of sinners. Don't condemn me along with murderers. Their hands are dirty with evil schemes, and they constantly take bribes. But I am not like that; I live with integrity. So redeem me and show me mercy. Now I stand on solid ground, and I will publicly praise the LORD.

Reflection

The Psalmist took a stand. In this stand, he declared who he would and would not associate with as well as his commitment to live with integrity, making public his faith in God. Where do you stand? What declaration will you make over your life today regarding how you will live? Utilize this Psalm as a springboard for your own declaration.

Prayer

You, Lord, are the foundation of my life upon which I stand. And, You are a sure and solid foundation. I declare today that I will live my life openly as a Christian doing my best to obey Your commands.

Day 23   **Declaration**

Trust

Psalm 146, NLT

Praise the LORD! Let all that I am praise the LORD. I will praise the LORD as long as I live. I will sing praises to my God with my dying breath. Don't put your confidence in powerful people; there is no help for you there. When they breathe their last, they return to the earth, and all their plans die with them. But joyful are those who have the God of Israel as their helper, whose hope is in the LORD their God. He made heaven and earth, the sea, and everything in them. He keeps every promise forever. He gives justice to the oppressed and food to the hungry. The LORD frees the prisoners. The LORD opens the eyes of the blind. The LORD lifts up those who are weighed down. The LORD loves the godly. The LORD protects the foreigners among us. He cares for the orphans and widows, but he frustrates the plans of the wicked. The LORD will reign forever. He will be your God, O Jerusalem, throughout the generations. Praise the LORD!

Reflection

Our confidence (or trust) is not to be in powerful people. Rather our trust needs to be in God. The Psalmist recounts the attributes of God (i.e. creator, promise keeper, etc.) thus giving reason for his confidence in Him. Take a moment and read back through today's Psalm making a list of all the attributes of God which you discover in the text. Then, take a moment to reflect on your own experience of God in these areas. End by making your own declaration of trust.

Prayer

Father, when I look at who You have revealed Yourself to be in Your Word and in my daily life, why would I ever consider putting my confidence in anyone or anything else. You alone are worthy. You alone are able. You alone are good. I choose to trust You with all of my heart.

Day 24   **Declaration**
Obedience

Psalm 119:57-64, NLT

LORD, you are mine! I promise to obey your words! With all my heart I want your blessings. Be merciful as you promised. I pondered the direction of my life, and I turned to follow your laws. I will hurry, without delay, to obey your commands. Evil people try to drag me into sin, but I am firmly anchored to your instructions. I rise at midnight to thank you for your just regulations. I am a friend to anyone who fears you — anyone who obeys your commandments. O LORD, your unfailing love fills the earth; teach me your decrees.

Reflection

So many people let life happen to them, living passively without thought to the direction they will go. Not so the Psalmist. Pondering his direction he made a proactive choice that he would obey God's commands. He even hurried to obey and anchored his life to God's Word. What would/does it look like to have your life anchored to His law? What will you declare about obedience today?

Prayer

Lord, I do not want to live passively by responding to life as it happens. Instead, I make a declaration that my decisions and actions will be a reflection of Your Word. I choose to obey You, anchoring myself to Your commands.

Part Four: The Climb

When the Israelites would go on pilgrimage to Jerusalem, they spoke of going "up" to Jerusalem because the city was situated on a hill. They had to climb up to it. They even had a series of Psalms which were known as the Songs of Ascent, which they would sing as they ascended to Jerusalem. And so, we embark on our climb. Our heart longs for Him. We have prepared for the journey. We have declared our faith. We now set our heart on pilgrimage.

Day 25   The Climb
Patience

Psalm 40, NLT

I waited patiently for the LORD to help me, and he turned to me and heard my cry. He lifted me out of the pit of despair, out of the mud and the mire. He set my feet on solid ground and steadied me as I walked along. He has given me a new song to sing, a hymn of praise to our God. Many will see what he has done and be amazed. They will put their trust in the LORD. Oh, the joys of those who trust the LORD, who have no confidence in the proud or in those who worship idols. O LORD my God, you have performed many wonders for us. Your plans for us are too numerous to list. You have no equal. If I tried to recite all your wonderful deeds, I would never come to the end of them. You take no delight in sacrifices or offerings. Now that you have made me listen, I finally understand — you don't require burnt offerings or sin offerings. Then I said, "Look, I have come. As is written about me in the Scriptures: I take joy in doing your will, my God, for your instructions are written on my heart."

I have told all your people about your justice. I have not been afraid to speak out, as you, O LORD, well know. I have not kept the good news of your justice hidden in my heart; I have talked about your faithfulness and saving power. I have told everyone in the great assembly of your unfailing love and faithfulness. LORD, don't hold back your tender mercies from me. Let your unfailing love and faithfulness always protect me. For troubles surround me — too many to count! My sins pile up so high I can't see my way out. They outnumber the hairs on my head. I have lost all courage. Please, LORD, rescue me! Come quickly, LORD, and help me. May those who try to destroy me be humiliated and put to shame. May those who take delight in my trouble be turned back in disgrace. Let them be horrified by their shame, for they said, "Aha! We've got him now!" But may all who search for you be filled with joy and gladness in you. May those who love your salvation repeatedly shout, "The LORD is great!" As for me, since I am poor and needy, let the Lord keep me in his thoughts. You are my helper and my savior. O my God, do not delay.

Reflection

In the New Testament book of Hebrews, we are told to emulate those who by faith and patience inherited the promises of God. We tend to like the faith part of that command but find ourselves unnerved when it comes to patience. After all we live in an instant society — who wants patience? But David knew the importance of being patient and waiting on God. By waiting patiently for God's timing and help, he experienced being lifted from the muddy pit of despair and being placed on solid ground. And through it all, God was honored and glorified as people were amazed at what God had done. You may not always understand the challenges you face in life. But you can be assured God hears your cry, is thinking about you and will rescue you. Wait patiently for Him and His timing. Take a moment to declare your commitment to patiently wait on God.

Prayer

There are times in life when I admit I do not understand Your timing, Lord. Patience is something I struggle with. Yet, in hindsight I have found that waiting on You is far better than taking matters into my own hands and trying to force things. Your timing is divine timing. I choose to wait on You, patiently trusting Your faithfulness.

Day 26   **The Climb**
Discipline

Psalm 15, NLT

Who may worship in your sanctuary, LORD? Who may enter your presence on your holy hill? Those who lead blameless lives and do what is right, speaking the truth from sincere hearts. Those who refuse to gossip or harm their neighbors or speak evil of their friends. Those who despise flagrant sinners, and honor the faithful followers of the LORD, and keep their promises even when it hurts. Those who lend money without charging interest, and who cannot be bribed to lie about the innocent. Such people will stand firm forever.

Reflection

Many people see the word discipline as a negative word. However, discipline brings freedom. For example, if you are undisciplined in your spending, you end up in financial ruin, but if you are disciplined, it leads to financial freedom. The process toward discipline begins with desire. We spent the first few days of this devotional focusing on desire as we sought God to stir up our longings for Him. With the longing of our heart clarified, we then made a decision to do something about it by spending a season in preparation with prayer, fasting and sacrifice. Now we are challenged to commit to discipline. In this Psalm, David listed some characteristics of a disciplined life which resulted in entering into God's presence and standing firm. Or, as The Message puts it, those who live this way get invited to God's place for dinner. What does it look like for you to live a disciplined life? What declaration will you make today regarding discipline?

Prayer

Lord, I have seen that when I live in an undisciplined manner my life gets messy and it does not honor You. In fact, I find myself in more bondage. But with discipline comes freedom. So today, I commit myself to discipline. Help me to be disciplined in my words, thoughts and actions.

Day 27   **The Climb**
Pilgrimage

Psalm 84, NLT

How lovely is your dwelling place, O LORD of Heaven's Armies. I long, yes, I faint with longing to enter the courts of the LORD. With my whole being, body and soul, I will shout joyfully to the living God. Even the sparrow finds a home, and the swallow builds her nest and raises her young at a place near your altar, O LORD of Heaven's Armies, my King and my God! What joy for those who can live in your house, always singing your praises. What joy for those whose strength comes from the LORD, who have set their minds on a pilgrimage to Jerusalem. When they walk through the Valley of Weeping, it will become a place of refreshing springs. The autumn rains will clothe it with blessings. They will continue to grow stronger, and each of them will appear before God in Jerusalem. O LORD God of Heaven's Armies, hear my prayer. Listen, O God of Jacob. O God, look with favor upon the king, our shield! Show favor to the one you have anointed. A single day in your courts is better than a thousand anywhere else! I would rather be a gatekeeper in the house of my God than live the good life in the homes of the wicked. For the LORD God is our sun and our shield. He gives us grace and glory. The LORD will withhold no good thing from those who do what is right. O LORD of Heaven's Armies, what joy for those who trust in you.

Reflection

The temple in Jerusalem was the center of the Jewish faith. Three times a year, the Israelites would make their pilgrimage to Jerusalem to celebrate the festival seasons. It was a time of joy and anticipation. Soon they would be in the presence of God in His holy temple. These festivals provided an opportunity for the community to reaffirm their commitment to God's covenant. As the people travelled, they would often sing the songs of ascent found in Psalms 120 – 134. Paul wrote that our bodies are now the temple of the Holy Spirit — God lives within us. As we set out on our pilgrimage, we are not going to a literal temple. Rather our pilgrimage is a pilgrimage of the heart as we prepare ourselves to meet the Lord at the cross and on Resurrection Sunday. And when we arrive, it will provide us with an opportunity to reaffirm our covenant with Him and to experience a renewal of our spirit — to be regenerated. What does it mean to have your heart set on pilgrimage? This Psalm basically answers that question. There is a passion and longing for God's presence. Even wildlife longed to set up residence in the house of God. Along the way difficulties would be encountered, yet God would turn it around so that even the difficult places would become a place of blessing. Rather than find themselves depleted by the journey, they would find themselves strengthened. In fact, verse five says they were already strong in the Lord and in verse seven we find that they have become stronger. Today, as you have walked through this process, you are stronger than you were twenty-seven days ago. And as you climb up the next thirteen days, you are going to go to a new level of strength in the Lord. Is your heart set on pilgrimage? Are you ready to climb?

Prayer

My heart is set on pilgrimage! I am excited to climb up to a new level in my walk with You, Lord. I am excited to come into Your presence and reconfirm my commitment to You. Lord, You have done so much in my life already during this process of regeneration, but I know You have more to do. So, I surrender to Your process.

Day 28   **The Climb**
Path

Psalm 1, NLT

Oh, the joys of those who do not follow the advice of the wicked, or stand around with sinners, or join in with mockers. But they delight in the law of the LORD, meditating on it day and night. They are like trees planted along the riverbank, bearing fruit each season. Their leaves never wither, and they prosper in all they do. But not the wicked! They are like worthless chaff, scattered by the wind. They will be condemned at the time of judgment. Sinners will have no place among the godly. For the LORD watches over the path of the godly, but the path of the wicked leads to destruction.

Reflection

The path we follow is a path where we delight in doing God's will. It is a path that is not well travelled. In fact, Jesus said the path was wide that leads to destruction but narrow that leads to life and that few find it. You have found the narrow path. It's a way of living that delights in doing things God's way. The world scoffs at it for the world delights in doing things its own way. But God's way is the way of life, vibrancy and fruitfulness. What does this path look like for you today? Do it with all your heart! Delight in the opportunity.

Prayer

Thank You for directing me to the narrow path. There is such joy being led by You along this journey. Show me the direction I need to take today. May my conversations and interactions with others be reflective of Your path.

Day 29   The Climb
Companions

Psalm 133, NLT
How wonderful and pleasant it is when brothers live together in harmony! For harmony is as precious as the anointing oil that was poured over Aaron's head, that ran down his beard and onto the border of his robe. Harmony is as refreshing as the dew from Mount Hermon that falls on the mountains of Zion. And there the LORD has pronounced his blessing, even life everlasting.

Reflection
The word harmony is often used when speaking of music. Musical harmony takes place when different yet complimenting notes are played or sung together at the same time. The melody on its own is nice but it lacks something. When harmony is added, a richness is provided. As the Israelites made their journey to Jerusalem, they were not alone, there were many pilgrims on the road traveling alongside them. These people had the same focus and the same destination. As they travelled together, camaraderie would be developed as they kept each other company, shared provisions and protected one another.

So also, you do not journey alone. How refreshing to be connected with other believers who are like-minded in their commitment to God. A solitary Christian is like a melody, nice but lacking something. But when Christians are connected in community, a richness is added. Our lives compliment and harmonize with one another. Who are your travelling companions? How have you experienced these relationships enriching your life? If you are not connected to other believers, what can you do to get connected?

Prayer

Lord, I am grateful that You have given me companions — that I am not alone on this journey. These friendships have enriched my life. As we move forward in this journey, may we harmonize with one another, living in unity. While I thank You for blessing me with their friendship, I ask that You would help me to be a blessing to them.

Day 30   **The Climb**
Steep

Psalm 121, NLT

I look up to the mountains — does my help come from there? My help comes from the LORD, who made heaven and earth! He will not let you stumble; the one who watches over you will not slumber. Indeed, he who watches over Israel never slumbers or sleeps. The LORD himself watches over you! The LORD stands beside you as your protective shade. The sun will not harm you by day, nor the moon at night. The LORD keeps you from all harm and watches over your life. The LORD keeps watch over you as you come and go, both now and forever.

Reflection

Sometimes the climb is steep and treacherous. The circumstances and situations we face in life can be precarious, making the journey difficult. But, God will not let us stumble. He watches over us with such care and concern. How encouraging to know He is always there and as Paul wrote in 1 Corinthians, nothing can ever separate us from His love. Are you currently in a hard place, facing some difficult decisions or challenging circumstances? Be encouraged that He is watching over you as you pour out your heart to Him.

Prayer

Lord, how reassuring to know that You will not allow me to stumble and fall. You keep me from evil and preserve my life. You know the situations I currently face. I look to You for You are my help for I know that nothing is too difficult for You. Guide my steps and watch over me I pray.

Day 31
Night

The Climb

Psalm 119:54-64, NLT

Your decrees have been the theme of my songs wherever I have lived. I reflect at night on who you are, O LORD; therefore, I obey your instructions. This is how I spend my life: obeying your commandments. LORD, you are mine! I promise to obey your words! With all my heart I want your blessings. Be merciful as you promised. I pondered the direction of my life, and I turned to follow your laws. I will hurry, without delay, to obey your commands. Evil people try to drag me into sin, but I am firmly anchored to your instructions. I rise at midnight to thank you for your just regulations. I am a friend to anyone who fears you — anyone who obeys your commandments. O LORD, your unfailing love fills the earth; teach me your decrees.

Reflection

Pilgrimages were quite often long journeys which would require spending many nights away from the safety of home. For many people, night can be a scary time, especially when out in the wilderness. Even in our modern world, people tend to experience more anxiety at night with many choosing to self-medicate to calm themselves down or perhaps utilize noise to drown out their fears. But, the Psalmist found the night hours to be a time to meditate upon God and His Word, even rising to give Him praise. As you journey, you may encounter a night time experience of the soul; a time when it is difficult to see and the terrors of the night surround you. But, God will be your peace. As you meditate upon God's character and Word, you will find your anxieties quieted. Also, be encouraged for in a short time the sun will rise and darkness will be dispelled.

Prayer

Lord, the night is no longer a time of fear, but rather a time to meditate upon You. You have dispelled my anxieties. I am at peace. Thank You for Your presence which sustains me.

Day 32   **The Climb**
Progress

Psalm 18, MSG

I love you, GOD — you make me strong. GOD is bedrock under my feet, the castle in which I live, my rescuing knight. My God — the high crag where I run for dear life, hiding behind the boulders, safe in the granite hideout. I sing to GOD, the Praise-Lofty, and find myself safe and saved. The hangman's noose was tight at my throat; devil waters rushed over me. Hell's ropes cinched me tight; death traps barred every exit. A hostile world! I call to GOD, I cry to God to help me. From his palace he hears my call; my cry brings me right into his presence — a private audience! Earth wobbles and lurches; huge mountains shake like leaves, Quake like aspen leaves because of his rage. His nostrils flare, bellowing smoke; his mouth spits fire. Tongues of fire dart in and out; he lowers the sky. He steps down; under his feet an abyss opens up. He's riding a winged creature, swift on wind-wings. Now he's wrapped himself in a trench coat of black-cloud darkness. But his cloud-brightness bursts through, spraying hailstones and fireballs. Then GOD thundered out of heaven; the High God gave a great shout, spraying hailstones and fireballs. God shoots his arrows — pandemonium! He hurls his lightnings — a rout! The secret sources of ocean are exposed, the hidden depths of earth lie uncovered The moment you roar in protest, let loose your hurricane anger. But me he caught — reached all the way from sky to sea; he pulled me out Of that ocean of hate, that enemy chaos, the void in which I was drowning. They hit me when I was down, but GOD stuck by me. He stood me up on a wide-open field; I stood there saved —

surprised to be loved! GOD made my life complete when I placed all the pieces before him. When I got my act together, he gave me a fresh start. Now I'm alert to GOD's ways; I don't take God for granted. Every day I review the ways he works; I try not to miss a trick. I feel put back together, and I'm watching my step. GOD rewrote the text of my life when I opened the book of my heart to his eyes. The good people taste your goodness, The whole people taste your health, The true people taste your truth, The bad ones can't figure you out. You take the side of the down-and-out, But the stuck-up you take down a peg. Suddenly, GOD, you floodlight my life; I'm blazing with glory, God's glory! I smash the bands of marauders, I vault the highest fences. What a God! His road stretches straight and smooth. Every GOD-direction is road-tested. Everyone who runs toward him Makes it. Is there any god like GOD? Are we not at bedrock? Is not this the God who armed me, then aimed me in the right direction? Now I run like a deer; I'm king of the mountain. He shows me how to fight; I can bend a bronze bow! You protect me with salvation-armor; you hold me up with a firm hand, caress me with your gentle ways. You cleared the ground under me so my footing was firm. When I chased my enemies I caught them; I didn't let go till they were dead men. I nailed them; they were down for good; then I walked all over them. You armed me well for this fight, you smashed the upstarts. You made my enemies turn tail, and I wiped out the haters. They cried "uncle" but Uncle didn't come; They yelled for GOD and got no for an answer. I ground them to dust; they gusted in the wind. I threw them out, like garbage in the gutter. You rescued me from a squabbling people; you made me a leader of nations. People I'd never heard of served me; the moment they got wind of me they listened. The foreign devils gave up; they came on their bellies, crawling from their hideouts. Live, GOD! Blessings from my Rock, my free and freeing God, towering! This God set things right for me and shut up the people who talked back. He rescued me from enemy anger, he pulled me from the grip of upstarts, He saved me from the bullies. That's why I'm thanking you, GOD, all over the world. That's why I'm singing songs that rhyme your name. God's king takes the trophy; God's chosen is beloved. I mean David and all his children — always.

Reflection

What an amazing scene David describes in this Psalm. God rescued him, put him back together and rewrote the text of his life. He was no longer who he used to be. His "now" is different from his past. Now I run like a deer. He now defeats his enemies.

The text of your life has also been rewritten. You are no longer who you used to be. In our day-to-day life, it is difficult to evaluate our progress but looking back over time our growth becomes more evident. This is very similar to being on a journey. One days walk may not be very far but when you keep walking for multiple days, over time you travel a long way. Look back over your journey. Where has God brought you from? Where and who are you now?

Prayer

Father, You have rewritten my life and I am so very grateful! When I look back over my journey, I am amazed at what You have brought me through. Your transforming power has done such a work that sometimes I don't recognize myself. You have made me strong and given me confidence. And as if that wasn't enough, You are still at work in my life taking me to new places. All praise to Your Name, God!

Day 33   **The Climb**
Worship

Psalm 122, NLT

I was glad when they said to me, "Let us go to the house of the LORD." And now here we are, standing inside your gates, O Jerusalem. Jerusalem is a well-built city; its seamless walls cannot be breached. All the tribes of Israel — the LORD's people — make their pilgrimage here. They come to give thanks to the name of the LORD, as the law requires of Israel. Here stand the thrones where judgment is given, the thrones of the dynasty of David. Pray for peace in Jerusalem. May all who love this city prosper. O Jerusalem, may there be peace within your walls and prosperity in your palaces. For the sake of my family and friends, I will say, "May you have peace." For the sake of the house of the LORD our God, I will seek what is best for you, O Jerusalem.

Reflection

How awesome it is to go to the house of the Lord. Of course, we realize the house of God is not the physical building. The house of God, the church, is the assembly of the people of God. We don't go to church. We are the church! There is something powerful about coming together with other believers for the purpose of worshiping God.

First, when we participate in corporate worship it honors God. With other believers, we proclaim His lordship, rulership and reign in our lives.

Second, it gets our mind off our momentary troubles and concerns and focuses our attention on the one who sits on the throne — the one who is able to do immeasurably more than we could ever ask or imagine. Our faith is built up as we recognize how big our God is.

Third, it is at the house of the Lord where we encourage one another in our faith. Our faith is nurtured and built up by the proclamation of the Word and interacting with other believers through conversation, laughter, serving and praying for one another.

Corporate worship is vital for the spiritual health of a believer! As you continue on your pilgrimage today, may your heart be filled with gladness as you go to the house of God.

Prayer

Father, I am excited to go to Your house to worship You today! I prepare my heart to proclaim Your rulership in my life. My desire is to honor and glorify You. Build up my faith today and use me to build up the faith of others. Strengthen me today for the journey which lies before me.

Day 34   The Climb
Wilderness

Psalm 91, NLT

Those who live in the shelter of the Most High will find rest in the shadow of the Almighty. This I declare about the LORD: He alone is my refuge, my place of safety; he is my God, and I trust him. For he will rescue you from every trap and protect you from deadly disease. He will cover you with his feathers. He will shelter you with his wings. His faithful promises are your armor and protection. Do not be afraid of the terrors of the night, nor the arrow that flies in the day. Do not dread the disease that stalks in darkness, nor the disaster that strikes at midday. Though a thousand fall at your side though ten thousand are dying around you, these evils will not touch you. Just open your eyes, and see how the wicked are punished. If you make the LORD your refuge, if you make the Most High your shelter, no evil will conquer you; no plague will come near your home. For he will order his angels to protect you wherever you go. They will hold you up with their hands so you won't even hurt your foot on a stone. You will trample upon lions and cobras; you will crush fierce lions and serpents under your feet! The LORD says, "I will rescue those who love me. I will protect those who trust in my name. When they call on me, I will answer; I will be with them in trouble. I will rescue and honor them. I will reward them with a long life and give them my salvation."

Reflection

Our pilgrimage takes us through a wild place — corporate jungles, cut-throat businesses, broken families, shady politics. It can be quite dangerous. But, His faithful promises are your armor and protection (Psalm 91:4). Wow! He is a promise keeping God, so when He said He will rescue us from every trap and protect us from the fatal plague, He meant it. What are you up against right now in your journey? What wild thing leers at you from the wilderness? God has even ordered His angels to protect you and has empowered you to walk on that which was out to destroy you. Prayerfully face those circumstances with faith, calling upon God and leaning upon His promises.

Prayer

Lord, I can hear the wild things which stalk me in the wilderness of life but I am not afraid for You are with me. I know You have sent Your angels to protect me. I know that You have given me the victory. So I choose to praise You in the midst of the wilderness.

Day 35   The Climb
Protection

Psalm 20, NIV

May the LORD answer you when you are in distress; may the name of the God of Jacob protect you. May he send you help from the sanctuary and grant you support from Zion. May he remember all your sacrifices and accept your burnt offerings. May he give you the desire of your heart and make all your plans succeed. May we shout for joy over your victory and lift up our banners in the name of our God. May the LORD grant all your requests. Now this I know: The LORD gives victory to his anointed. He answers him from his heavenly sanctuary with the victorious power of his right hand. Some trust in chariots and some in horses, but we trust in the name of the LORD our God. They are brought to their knees and fall, but we rise up and stand firm. LORD, give victory to the king! Answer us when we call!

Reflection

Today's reading was a short Psalm, yet filled with many blessings. May the Lord answer you, protect you, send you help, grant you support, remember your sacrifices, accept your offerings, give you your heart's desire, make all your plans succeed and grant all your requests. God is your protector and you will walk in victory. Trust in Him! Which of the blessings in this Psalm do you need to personally receive today? Use your time of prayer to claim these blessings.

Prayer

Lord, You are such an amazing God. You are so good to me. I choose to put my trust in You for You are faithful and will accomplish all You have promised. By faith, I receive Your blessings today.

Day 36   The Climb
Fatigue

Psalm 23, NLT

The LORD is my shepherd; I have all that I need. He lets me rest in green meadows; he leads me beside peaceful streams. He renews my strength. He guides me along right paths, bringing honor to his name. Even when I walk through the darkest valley, I will not be afraid, for you are close beside me. Your rod and your staff protect and comfort me. You prepare a feast for me in the presence of my enemies. You honor me by anointing my head with oil. My cup overflows with blessings. Surely your goodness and unfailing love will pursue me all the days of my life, and I will live in the house of the LORD forever.

Reflection

As we travel on this journey, we undoubtedly encounter times where we grow weary. How encouraging to remember that the Lord is our shepherd. He provides for our needs. He gives us rest. He renews our strength. What do you need from Him today? Allow your shepherd to lead you and be refreshed.

Prayer

Father, You are the Good Shepherd. You are the one who provides for my needs and in Your compassion You bring me rest. It is so encouraging to know that Your goodness and unfailing love pursue me. I can't get away from them! Thank You for refreshing me today.

Day 37   **The Climb**
Perspective

Psalm 73, NLT

Truly God is good to Israel, to those whose hearts are pure. But as for me, I almost lost my footing. My feet were slipping, and I was almost gone. For I envied the proud when I saw them prosper despite their wickedness. They seem to live such painless lives; their bodies are so healthy and strong. They don't have troubles like other people; they're not plagued with problems like everyone else. They wear pride like a jeweled necklace and clothe themselves with cruelty. These fat cats have everything their hearts could ever wish for! They scoff and speak only evil; in their pride they seek to crush others. They boast against the very heavens, and their words strut throughout the earth. And so the people are dismayed and confused, drinking in all their words. "What does God know?" they ask. "Does the Most High even know what's happening?" Look at these wicked people — enjoying a life of ease while their riches multiply. Did I keep my heart pure for nothing? Did I keep myself innocent for no reason? I get nothing but trouble all day long; every morning brings me pain. If I had really spoken this way to others, I would have been a traitor to your people. So I tried to understand why the wicked prosper. But what a difficult task it is! Then I went into your sanctuary, O God, and I finally understood the destiny of the wicked. Truly, you put them on a slippery path and send them sliding over the cliff to destruction. In an instant they are destroyed, completely swept away by terrors. When you arise, O Lord, you will laugh at their silly ideas as a person laughs at dreams in the morning. Then I realized that my heart was bitter, and I was all torn up inside. I was so foolish and ignorant — I must have seemed like a senseless animal to you. Yet I still belong to you; you hold my right hand. You guide me with your counsel, leading me to a glorious destiny. Whom have I in heaven but you? I desire you more than anything on earth. My health may fail, and my spirit may grow weak, but God remains the strength of my heart; he is mine forever. Those who desert him will perish, for you destroy those who abandon you. But as for me, how good it is to be near God! I have made the Sovereign LORD my shelter, and I will tell everyone about the wonderful things you do.

Reflection

Perspective is interesting. At ground level, we see our surroundings one way. But when we begin to gain altitude, (i.e. the view from a mountain top, the view out of the window of an airborne plane) the same location looks far different. From a greater height, you see a bigger picture which puts things into perspective.

Asaph almost slipped off the edge of the cliff on his journey. For a season, he lost his perspective. Distracted by the prosperity of the wicked, he failed to see the big picture. But when he went into the sanctuary, he regained his focus and saw things for what they truly were.

The view of the world in which we live can be deceptive. From the world's perspective, it may look like our journey has been in vain. But when we step back to look at the big picture, it all comes into focus. How is your perspective? Paul tells us in Galatians to not grow weary in doing good for we will reap a harvest if we do not give up. Do not give up — keep climbing!

Prayer

Lord, help me to keep the big picture in mind as I make my way on this journey. I don't want to get distracted by what appears to be the prosperity of the wicked. Today, I recognize two truths. First, the only sure way is Your way. Second, when I live my life for You, it is not lived in vain. So, I will not grow weary in doing good. I will press on!

Day 38   The Climb
Cross

Psalm 130, NLT

From the depths of despair, O LORD, I call for your help. Hear my cry, O Lord. Pay attention to my prayer. LORD, if you kept a record of our sins, who, O Lord, could ever survive? But you offer forgiveness, that we might learn to fear you. I am counting on the LORD; yes, I am counting on him. I have put my hope in his word. I long for the Lord more than sentries long for the dawn, yes, more than sentries long for the dawn. O Israel, hope in the LORD; for with the LORD there is unfailing love. His redemption overflows. He himself will redeem Israel from every kind of sin.

Reflection

Today is Good Friday, and we have arrived at our destination. This is the place where history was made. It was at the cross that the debt of our sin was paid with the currency of His blood. Without His sacrifice, we would have no hope. Because of His sacrifice, we have been forgiven, set free from our past and gifted with a vibrant, purposeful life. Today, we remember what a terrific price Christ paid. Use your time today to reaffirm your need for the Lord and your commitment to Him. If there is anything you are still hanging on to (i.e. shame, guilt, bitterness, fear) leave it at the cross today.

Prayer

How good it is to stand at the cross and remember all that You have done for me. You paid the price for all my shame and guilt and it cost You Your life. I didn't deserve for You to do this for me. But, You willingly gave Yourself because You loved me. And, by Your grace I have been saved. I reaffirm my commitment to You. I am Your servant. You are my Lord.

Day 39   The Climb
Quietness

Psalm 131, NLT

LORD, my heart is not proud; my eyes are not haughty. I don't concern myself with matters too great or too awesome for me to grasp. Instead, I have calmed and quieted myself, like a weaned child who no longer cries for its mother's milk. Yes, like a weaned child is my soul within me. O Israel, put your hope in the LORD — now and always.

Reflection

We are at the place between the death of Christ and His resurrection. For those who lived at the time of Christ and followed Him, it would have been a day of mourning. They did not realize that on the next day their Lord would return to them. But we know that tomorrow is Resurrection Day, and so we wait with anticipation. While we wait, our heart is at peace, content like a child who has been comforted by his mother. Reflect today on the peace and comfort God has brought into your life through your relationship with Jesus.

Prayer

Lord Jesus, You are the author of peace. You have made my life complete and I find myself fully content in You. I wait with anticipation to celebrate Your resurrection tomorrow.

Day 40   The Climb
Resurrection

Psalm 126, MSG

It seemed like a dream, too good to be true, when GOD returned Zion's exiles. We laughed, we sang, we couldn't believe our good fortune. We were the talk of the nations — "GOD was wonderful to them!" GOD was wonderful to us; we are one happy people. And now, GOD, do it again — bring rains to our drought-stricken lives So those who planted their crops in despair will shout hurrahs at the harvest, So those who went off with heavy hearts will come home laughing, with armloads of blessing.

Reflection

Happy Resurrection Day! For His disciples, the day Jesus was resurrected seemed like a dream, too good to be true. But, God was wonderful to them. God has been wonderful to us and we are one happy people! His resurrected life has given us abundant life. What has God done in your life during these last forty days? If you have been keeping a journal, review what you have written so that you can see the big picture. Perhaps you will find the following things to be true: The longing of your heart to know God was stirred up and is being filled. You eagerly sought God through prayer, fasting and sacrifice and you have found Him. You made declarations of your faith which have strengthened your resolve to follow Him. And now, you have climbed up to the place of His death and resurrection and discovered some things along the way. You have come to delight in God's path. You've been blessed with believing friends who travel this journey with you. You realize that God is with you, never letting you stumble, always watching out for you and that He has rewritten the text of your life! You started the climb strong but now you are stronger. You have been regenerated. Spring is here and a new season of fruitfulness lies ahead. While these forty days have been highly focused, it doesn't stop here. Keep implementing what you have learned. When people are recruited into the armed forces, their first stop is boot camp which is an intense season of training, preparing them to be successful soldiers. Boot camps are also found in the fitness world, supporting people who have not been physically active to acquire the discipline and skills necessary to lead a healthy lifestyle. Through this journey, you have acquired and/or sharpened some spiritual habits which have prepared you for where God wants to lead you next. Stay consistent with these disciplines of reading the Bible, prayer, worship, sacrifice and giving. You are positioned to be fruitful on behalf of the Kingdom of God — the Holy Spirit working through you as you are intimately connected to Him. Press on!

Prayer

Jesus, it seems too good to be true, but it is true. Death could not hold You. You are resurrected and are alive! You have also regenerated my life! I have encountered You Lord in a new and fresh way and Your resurrected life lives in me. You have blessed me and strengthened me. Lord, I worship You! You are amazing. As I venture on from here, I want to follow Your leading. I am Your servant. Use me as a conduit of Your love and grace so that others might know You in the way I have come to know You. Glorify Yourself in and through me I pray. In Jesus mighty Name, Amen.